PRENTICE HALL

Civics

Government and Economics in Action

TEST PREP

Richard Aucli

PEARSON

Boston, Massachusetts
Glenview, Illinois
Parsippany, New Jersey
Shoreview, Minnesota
Upper Saddle River, New Jersey

13-digit ISBN 978-0-13-365184-3
10-digit ISBN 0-13-365184-3

Aucli

Contents

Taking Tests

Do you panic at the thought of taking a standardized test? Here are some tips that most test developers recommend to help you achieve good scores.

MULTIPLE-CHOICE QUESTIONS

Read each part of a multiple-choice question to make sure you understand what is being asked.

Many tests are made up of multiple-choice questions. Some multiple-choice items are **direct questions.** They are complete sentences followed by possible answers, called distractors.

Direct Question	What is a narrow strip of land that has water on both sides and joins two larger bodies of land called?
The **distractors** list the possible answers.	**A** a bay **B** an isthmus **C** a lake **D** an island
TIP▸ Try each distractor as an answer to your question. Rule out the ones that don't work.	You can rule out A and C because they are bodies of water, not land. You can rule out D because an island is completely surrounded by water.

Other multiple-choice questions are **incomplete sentences** that you are to finish. They are followed by possible answers.

The **stem** tells you what the question is looking for	A narrow strip of land that has water on both sides and joins two larger bodies of land is called
Distractors	**A** a bay **B** an isthmus **C** a lake **D** an island
TIP▸ Turn the stem into a direct question, using *who, what, when, where,* or *why.*	What is a narrow strip of land that has water on both sides and joins two larger bodies of land called?

WHAT'S BEING TESTED?

Identify the type of question you are being asked.

Social studies tests often ask questions that involve reading comprehension. Other questions may require you to gather or interpret information from a map, graph, or chart. The following strategies will help you answer different kinds of questions.

Reading Comprehension Questions

What to do:	How to do it:
1. Determine the content and organization of the selection.	Read the **title.** Skim the selection. Look for key words that indicate time, cause-and-effect, or comparison.
2. Analyze the questions. Do they ask you to *recall facts?*	Look for **key words** in the stem: According to the selection . . . The selection states that . . .
Do they ask you to *make judgments?*	The main idea of the selection is . . . The author would likely agree that . . .
3. Read the selection.	Read quickly. Keep the questions in mind.
4. Answer the questions.	Try out each distractor and choose the best answer. Refer back to the selection if necessary.

Example:

A Region of Diversity The Khmer empire was one of many kingdoms in Southeast Asia. Unlike the Khmer empire, however, the other kingdoms were small because Southeast Asia's mountains kept people protected and apart. People had little contact with those who lived outside their own valley.

Why were most kingdoms in Southeast Asia small?

A disease killed many people
B lack of food
C climate was too hot
D mountains kept people apart

TIP▸ The key word because tells why the kingdoms were small.

(The correct answer is D.)

WHAT'S BEING TESTED?

(continued)

Map Questions

What to do:

1. Determine what kind of information is presented on the map.

How to do it:

Read the map **title.** It will indicate the purpose of the map.
Study the **map key.** It will explain the symbols used on the map.
Look at the **scale.** It will help you calculate distance between places on the map.

2. Read the question. Determine which component on the map will help you find the answer.

Look for **key words** in the stem.
About <u>how far</u> . . . [use the scale]
<u>What crops</u> were grown in . . . [use the map key]

3. Look at the map and answer the question in your own words.

Do not read the distractors yet.

4. Choose the best answer.

Decide which distractor agrees with the answer you determined from the map.

Eastern Europe: Language Groups

In which of these countries are Thraco-Illyrian languages spoken?

A Romania
B Albania
C Hungary
D Lithuania

TIP▶ Read the labels and the key to understand the map.
(The correct answer is B.)

Graph Questions

What to do:	How to do it:
1. Determine the purpose of the graph.	Read the graph **title.** It indicates what the graph represents.
2. Determine what information on the graph will help you find the answer.	Read the **labels** on the graph or on the key. They tell the units of measurement used by the graph.
3. Choose the best answer.	Decide which distractor agrees with the answer you determined from the graph.

Example

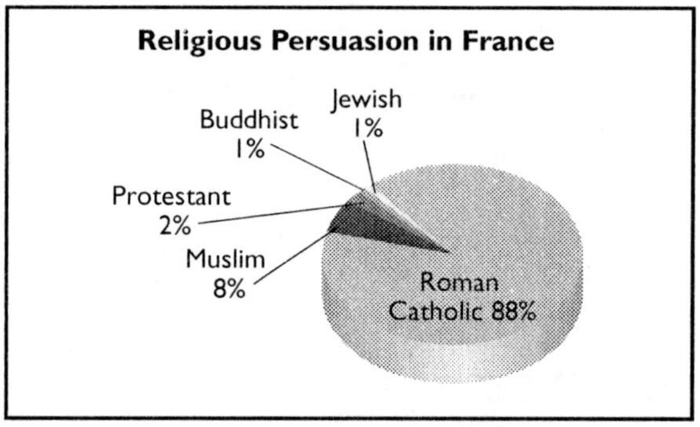

A **Circle graph** shows the relationship of parts to the whole in terms of percentages.

After Roman Catholics, the next largest religious population in France is

A Buddhist **C** Jewish
B Protestant **D** Muslim

TIP▶ Compare the percentages listed in the labels.
(The correct answer is D.)

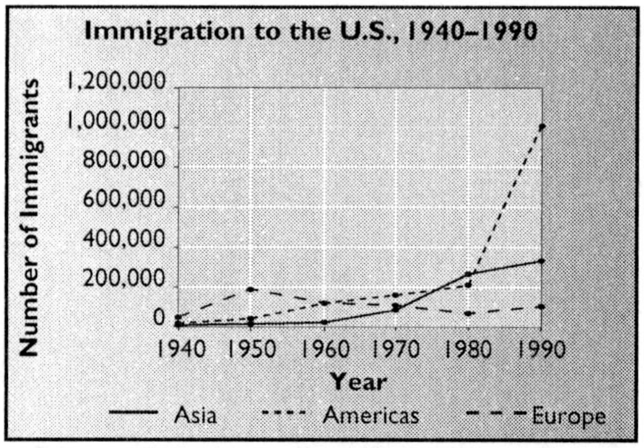

A **line graph** shows a pattern or change over time by the direction of the line.

Between 1980 and 1990, immigration to the U.S. from the Americas

A decreased a little **C** stayed about the same
B increased greatly **D** increased a little

TIP▶ Compare the vertical distance between the two correct points on the line graph.
(The correct answer is B.)

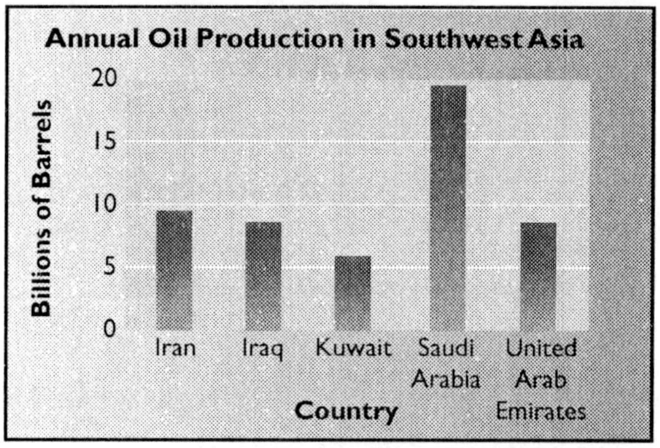

A **bar graph** compares differences in quantity by showing bars of different lengths.

Saudi Arabia produces about how many more billions of barrels of oil a year than Iran?

A 5 billion **C** 15 billion
B 10 billion **D** 20 billion

TIP▶ Compare the heights of the bars to find the difference.
(The correct answer is B.)

_____ 7. The idea of direct democracy came from
A. the Magna Carta.
B. colonial newspapers.
C. ancient Athens.
D. Roman law.

_____ 8. A town meeting is an example of
A. representative democracy.
B. direct democracy.
C. a tyranny.
D. a republic.

_____ 9. The Magna Carta is still important today because
A. it was an important step toward establishing rights that no government can take away.
B. it is England's constitution.
C. it lists the rights of England's kings and queens.
D. it still protects the English nobles.

_____ 10. Tyranny refers to
A. a strong central government.
B. a government that abuses its power.
C. a government controlled by citizens.
D. a powerful monarchy.

_____ 11. Which was NOT a reason for revising the Articles of Confederation?
A. Congress had already agreed on a new form of government.
B. Congress could not enforce the laws.
C. Congress could not settle disputes between states.
D. Congress could not tax.

_____ 12. Madison's plan for government
A. was rejected almost immediately.
B. was especially popular with the smaller states.
C. seemed too weak to many delegates.
D. created a strong central government.

_____ 13. On the question of the slave trade, the delegates
A. agreed that each state should end it by 1808.
B. agreed to end it in 1808.
C. agreed that the national government could not end it before 1808.
D. could not reach agreement.

_____ **14.** The Great Compromise

A. was never adopted by the delegates.
B. established a two-house legislature.
C. won by a huge majority of the votes at the Constitutional Convention.
D. showed the weaknesses of the Constitutional Convention.

_____ **15.** In order for the Constitution to go into effect it had to be approved by

A. at least nine state conventions.
B. at least nine state legislatures.
C. the Continental Congress.
D. the President.

_____ **16.** Which of the following is NOT a goal set forth in the Preamble to the Constitution?

A. to promote the general welfare
B. to create a bicameral legislature
C. to provide for the common defense
D. to establish justice

_____ **17.** Under federalism,

A. state and federal governments have some shared and some separate powers.
B. the federal government decides what powers the states have.
C. the states can check the power of the federal government.
D. state and federal governments have completely different powers.

_____ **18.** Separation of powers means that

A. the judicial branch decides the powers of the other branches.
B. state and federal governments have different powers.
C. power is divided among the three branches of government.
D. each branch can limit the powers of the other branches.

_____ **19.** Which of the following is NOT true about amending the Constitution?

A. Every amendment must be ratified by three fourths of the state legislatures.
B. An amendment may be proposed by a national convention called by two thirds of the state legislatures.
C. Every amendment must be approved at both the national and state levels.
D. Congress may propose an amendment by two-thirds vote in both houses.

_____ **20.** The main argument in favor of the Bill of Rights was that it would

A. make the Constitution more like the Magna Carta.
B. win more public support for the new government.
C. test whether the amendment process worked.
D. limit the constitutional powers of the federal government.

_____ **21.** The main argument against the Bill of Rights was that
- **A.** it was not needed.
- **B.** the people did not approve of it.
- **C.** protecting citizens' rights should be up to the states.
- **D.** it limited the power of the government too much.

_____ **22.** People who "take the Fifth"
- **A.** have to tell the truth even if it will send them to jail.
- **B.** are using their constitutional right to remain silent.
- **C.** misunderstand the Constitution.
- **D.** are admitting their guilt.

_____ **23.** The rights of the accused do NOT include
- **A.** the right to a secret trial.
- **B.** the right to a speedy public trial.
- **C.** the right to remain silent.
- **D.** the right to question witnesses.

_____ **24.** In the *Tinker* case, the Supreme Court ruled that
- **A.** armbands may be regulated by a school principal.
- **B.** armbands are a form of speech protected by the First Amendment.
- **C.** schools are not places for political demonstrations.
- **D.** political armbands disrupt classes and may not be worn.

_____ **25.** Protecting the rights of citizens is
- **A.** easy to do since the Bill of Rights was passed.
- **B.** taken care of by the Bill of Rights.
- **C.** the job of the Supreme Court.
- **D.** a responsibility that all Americans share.

_____ **26.** Which of the following statements is NOT true about slavery in the early days of our nation?
- **A.** Both northern and southern states were satisfied with the compromise over slavery.
- **B.** It was important to the economy of many states.
- **C.** The people on both sides of the issue felt strongly about slavery.
- **D.** Northern and southern states compromised about it in order to ratify the Constitution.

_____ **27.** The Missouri Compromise
- **A.** divided new lands into "slave" and "free" territories.
- **B.** was the result of the Dred Scott decision.
- **C.** was forced on the South.
- **D.** satisfied both sides in the slavery debate.

_____ **28.** The Thirteenth Amendment
- **A.** made African Americans citizens of the states in which they lived.
- **B.** gave African American men the right to vote.
- **C.** was overturned by a later amendment.
- **D.** abolished slavery.

_____ **29.** The Fourteenth Amendment
- **A.** gave African American men the right to vote.
- **B.** abolished slavery.
- **C.** was found unconstitutional.
- **D.** gave citizenship to African Americans born in the United States.

_____ **30.** The Fifteenth Amendment
- **A.** made African Americans citizens of the states in which they lived.
- **B.** made segregation illegal.
- **C.** gave African American men the right to vote.
- **D.** abolished slavery.

_____ **31.** The Twenty-fourth Amendment
- **A.** gave African American women the right to vote.
- **B.** declared that citizens do not have to pay a tax to vote.
- **C.** has not yet been passed.
- **D.** gave African Americans equal protection of the laws.

_____ **32.** Women gained suffrage
- **A.** from the Bill of Rights.
- **B.** from the Fifteenth Amendment.
- **C.** from the Nineteenth Amendment.
- **D.** from the Twenty-fourth Amendment.

_____ **33.** The Twenty-sixth Amendment granted the right to vote to
- **A.** all women.
- **B.** people between 18 and 21 years of age.
- **C.** immigrants.
- **D.** African American women.

_____ **34.** The amendments to the Constitution are evidence that the Constitution
- **A.** is flexible.
- **B.** changes only in wartime.
- **C.** is finally perfect.
- **D.** gives the people too much power.

_____ **35.** The Supreme Court
- **A.** must be obeyed except by the President.
- **B.** can change the Constitution.
- **C.** has the final say over whether a law is constitutional.
- **D.** cannot overturn its earlier decisions.

_____ **36.** Excerpt 4 says that the people of the United States
- **A.** will create a new monarchy.
- **B.** declare their independence.
- **C.** intend to go to war against Great Britain to gain independence.
- **D.** ally themselves with Great Britain.

Name ______________________ Date ________________ Class __________

Unit 3 The Federal Government

Multiple Choice

Identify the letter of the choice that best completes the statement or answers the question.

_____ **1.** Which of the following statements is NOT true about Congress?
- **A.** Its main job is to make laws.
- **B.** It is the legislative branch of the government.
- **C.** It is made up of the House of Representatives and the Senate.
- **D.** It can appoint federal judges.

_____ **2.** Constituents, political parties, and lobbyists are similar in that they
- **A.** are illegal.
- **B.** work full time to try to influence members of Congress.
- **C.** put the needs of the whole nation ahead of local needs.
- **D.** want members of Congress to support their interests.

_____ **3.** When deciding how to vote, a member of Congress should consider all of the following EXCEPT
- **A.** the party's position.
- **B.** his or her own conscience.
- **C.** how much he or she will be paid.
- **D.** what constituents want.

_____ **4.** Congressional staff members do NOT include
- **A.** administrative assistants.
- **B.** lobbyists.
- **C.** caseworkers.
- **D.** legislative assistants.

_____ **5.** The number of representatives from a state
- **A.** does not change.
- **B.** can change after a census.
- **C.** is determined by the majority party.
- **D.** can never be more than 45.

_____ **6.** Senators
- **A.** represent an entire state.
- **B.** must have been born in the United States.
- **C.** serve the same length term as Representatives.
- **D.** do not have to worry about what people in their states think.

_____ **7.** The powers of Congress
- **A.** are given to it by state legislatures.
- **B.** are unlimited.
- **C.** are based on the goals of the Constitution.
- **D.** are limited to making laws.

_____ **8.** Congress does NOT have the power
A. to regulate commerce with other countries.
B. to declare laws unconstitutional.
C. to declare war.
D. to spend money.

_____ **9.** The elastic clause in the Constitution
A. gives Congress room to expand its powers.
B. sets strict limits on the powers of Congress.
C. gives Congress unlimited powers.
D. has been found unconstitutional.

_____ **10.** Cloture means that
A. an official count of the population has been taken.
B. the Senate has agreed to end debate on a bill.
C. a congressional committee is going to debate a bill.
D. the President has not signed a bill before Congress ends its session.

_____ **11.** The President
A. sets goals and develops policies for the nation.
B. is responsible for making laws.
C. is the head of the legislative branch of the government.
D. represents only voters.

_____ **12.** The President's power is limited in all of the following ways EXCEPT
A. Congress has the power to make the laws.
B. the Supreme Court can declare that a presidential act is unconstitutional.
C. the President can play only the roles mentioned in the Constitution.
D. a President can serve two terms.

_____ **13.** Which presidential role is NOT identified in the Constitution?
A. commander in chief
B. chief of state
C. chief diplomat
D. chief executive

_____ **14.** Making foreign policy is an example of the President's role as
A. chief diplomat.
B. chief executive.
C. legislative leader.
D. party leader.

_____ **15.** In order to turn policies into laws, the President may do all of the following EXCEPT

A. recommend possible laws.

B. introduce bills in Congress.

C. ask members of Congress to vote for bills.

D. urge the public to let Congress know they agree with the President.

_____ **16.** The President's judicial powers do NOT include

A. declaring laws unconstitutional.

B. pardoning convicted criminals.

C. reducing the punishment of convicted criminals.

D. appointing federal judges.

_____ **17.** Which of the following presidential appointments does NOT need the approval of Congress?

A. Secretary of State

B. Supreme Court justice

C. ambassador

D. White House chief of staff

_____ **18.** The Vice President

A. is appointed by the President.

B. presides over the House of Representatives.

C. may act as President if the President is seriously ill.

D. does not need to be as qualified as the President.

_____ **19.** The executive branch does NOT have the main responsibility for

A. enforcing laws.

B. turning policy into laws.

C. finding ways to carry out laws.

D. making policy.

_____ **20.** The President

A. has a good deal of freedom in spite of checks and balances.

B. has the right to keep all information secret from Congress and the courts.

C. cannot act in a crisis without the consent of Congress.

D. can order the government to take private property in a national emergency.

_____ **21.** All American courts, at every level,

A. determine whether a person is innocent or guilty.

B. settle disagreements between individuals.

C. decide whether an action is constitutional.

D. apply the law to an actual situation.

_____ **22.** A court can interpret a law
A. whenever the President asks it to.
B. whenever it wants to establish a precedent.
C. only in a specific case.
D. whenever Congress asks it to.

_____ **23.** Federal courts hear all of the following kinds of cases EXCEPT
A. disputes involving a foreign government.
B. cases affirmed in state appeals courts.
C. disputes about the meaning of the Constitution.
D. disputes between states.

_____ **24.** Which of the following courts NEVER have original jurisdiction?
A. United States courts of appeals
B. United States district courts
C. state trial courts
D. the United States Supreme Court

_____ **25.** Which of the following statements is NOT true of federal judges?
A. They are appointed for life.
B. They represent voters' interests.
C. Their decisions can have far-reaching results.
D. Their decisions can affect the meaning of laws.

_____ **26.** Who has the final say about what the Constitution means?
A. the Supreme Court
B. Congress
C. the President
D. all three government branches

_____ **27.** *Marbury* v. *Madison* established
A. judicial review.
B. limits on the presidency.
C. Congress's right to make laws.
D. the federal court system.

_____ **28.** Supreme Court decisions require a
A. unanimous vote.
B. two-thirds vote.
C. three-fourths vote.
D. simple majority vote.

_____ **29.** Supreme Court justices should NOT be influenced by
A. the Constitution.
B. what Congress had in mind when making a law.
C. what the President wants.
D. decisions of previous courts.

_____ **30.** A Supreme Court decision can be overturned by
A. public opinion.
B. a presidential veto.
C. a vote of Congress.
D. a constitutional amendment.

Interpreting Maps

Use the map below to choose the letter of the best answer.

Congressional Apportionment, 2003–2013

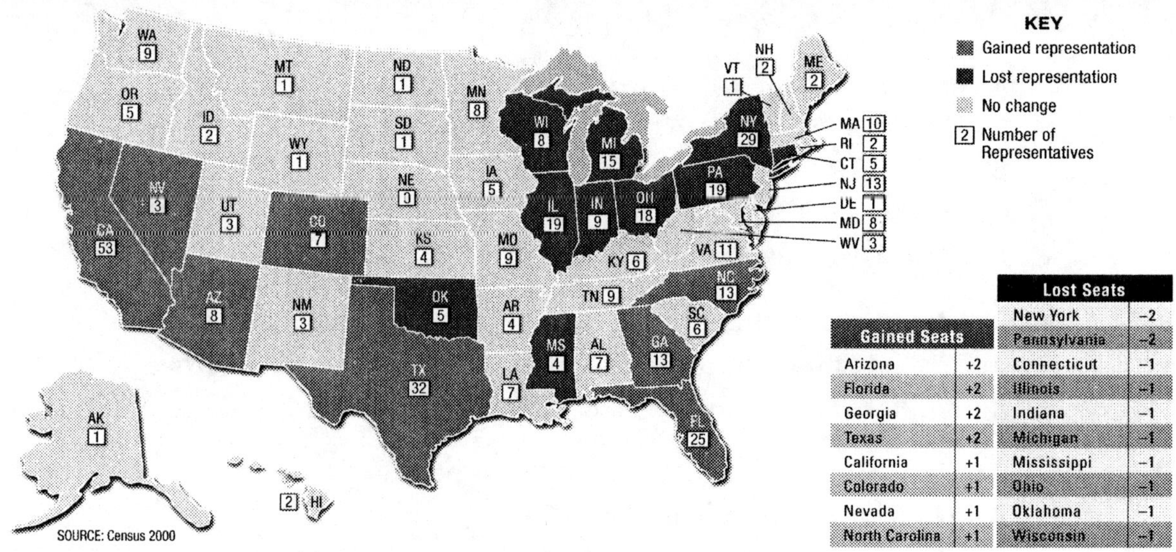

Gained Seats	
Arizona	+2
Florida	+2
Georgia	+2
Texas	+2
California	+1
Colorado	+1
Nevada	+1
North Carolina	+1

Lost Seats	
New York	–2
Pennsylvania	–2
Connecticut	–1
Illinois	–1
Indiana	–1
Michigan	–1
Mississippi	–1
Ohio	–1
Oklahoma	–1
Wisconsin	–1

_____ **31.** The map shows
- **A.** the number of people who live in each state.
- **B.** the total population of the United States.
- **C.** changes in House representation.
- **D.** the location of House districts in the states.

_____ **32.** Which statement about the map is NOT true?
- **A.** Some states gained seats in the House of Representatives.
- **B.** Some states lost seats in the House of Representatives.
- **C.** The total number of seats in the House of Representatives increased.
- **D.** Some states kept the same number of seats in the House of Representatives.

_____ **33.** The parts of the United States that gained the most seats are the
- **A.** southwest and northwest.
- **B.** southeast and southwest.
- **C.** northeast and southeast.
- **D.** northwest and northeast.

_____ **34.** The state with the most seats is located in
- **A.** the southeast.
- **B.** the west.
- **C.** the northeast.
- **D.** the east.

_____ **35.** The state with the second largest number of seats
- **A.** has the largest area.
- **B.** gained the most seats.
- **C.** gained two seats.
- **D.** lost the most seats.

Name ______________________ Date __________________ Class ___________

Unit 4 State and Local Government

Multiple Choice

Identify the letter of the choice that best completes the statement or answers the question.

_____ **1.** All of the following are true about the powers of state government EXCEPT

A. states alone have the power to set up public school systems.

B. none are shared with the national government.

C. the U.S. Constitution does not specifically list them.

D. they are part of the compromise called federalism.

_____ **2.** State constitutions

A. were models for the national Constitution.

B. are less detailed than the national Constitution.

C. usually do not include a bill of rights.

D. cannot be amended.

_____ **3.** Changes to state constitutions

A. usually are not necessary.

B. are made more often than changes to the national Constitution.

C. can only be made by state legislatures.

D. do not require voter approval in most states.

_____ **4.** A common argument for strong state governments is that, compared to the federal government, they are

A. less corrupt.

B. more likely to provide equal opportunities.

C. better able to solve problems involving many states.

D. better able to serve their citizens' needs.

_____ **5.** Seats in state legislatures are apportioned on the basis of the

A. wealth of the districts.

B. needs of the districts.

C. area of the districts.

D. population of the districts.

_____ **6.** One main difference between state legislatures and Congress is that

A. state legislatures cannot propose constitutional amendments.

B. state legislators are appointed by the governor.

C. citizens in some states can propose and pass laws.

D. all state legislators are volunteers.

_____ **7.** Most state tax revenue comes from
A. excise and property taxes.
B. sales and excise taxes.
C. income and sales taxes.
D. property and income taxes.

_____ **8.** The greatest source of executive power is the governor's
A. role as commander in chief of the National Guard.
B. power to enforce laws.
C. power to change the state constitution.
D. budget-making role.

_____ **9.** All state court judges
A. are chosen under the Missouri Plan.
B. serve for life if they are able.
C. have duties similar to those of federal judges.
D. are elected.

_____ **10.** Local governments are created by
A. the state government.
B. the local voters.
C. the U.S. Constitution.
D. a board of supervisors.

_____ **11.** The government closest to a direct democracy is the
A. county commission.
B. state legislature.
C. town meeting.
D. board of supervisors.

_____ **12.** A school district is an example of a
A. zoning law.
B. special district.
C. municipality.
D. ordinance.

_____ **13.** The weak-mayor plan
A. gives executive power to the city manager.
B. gives both legislative and executive power to a council.
C. is one type of commission plan.
D. requires direct election of the mayor by voters.

_____ **14.** Local governments spend the most money on
A. schools.
B. roads.
C. jails.
D. parks.

_____ **15.** Education is paid for by
A. state governments.
B. local, state, and federal governments.
C. local governments.
D. local government and the federal government.

_____ **16.** Zoning is the power of local government to

A. make rules for land use.

B. provide for public safety.

C. divide power among city, state, and federal governments.

D. make sure that restaurants meet health standards.

_____ **17.** A job of the local planning commission is to

A. decide what form of government a city should have.

B. set a city's spending goals.

C. attract new businesses to a community.

D. set goals for land use.

_____ **18.** To pay for the services they provide, local governments

A. can never collect income taxes.

B. can collect any taxes they want.

C. depend entirely on property taxes.

D. depend on state and federal funds.

_____ **19.** Which is NOT a way that local governments cooperate?

A. providing emergency services

B. operating jails

C. building hospitals

D. combining their city councils

_____ **20.** Local, state, and federal governments disagree about all of the following EXCEPT

A. who will decide what kinds of services to provide.

B. how to spend grant money.

C. that no one level of government can meet all citizens' needs.

D. who will pay for services.

_____ **21.** The governors in many states have less power than the President to

A. make the budget.

B. influence lawmaking.

C. veto bills.

D. appoint top executive branch officials.

_____ **22.** The first unit of local government to form in the colonies was the

A. special district.

B. city.

C. township.

D. county.

Analyzing Statistical Tables

Use the table below to choose the best answer.

Governments in the United States			
Type of government	**Number of governments**	**Number of elected officials**	**Average number of officials per government**
Federal	1	542	542
State	50	18,828	377
Local	84,995	493,830	6
County	3,043	58,818	19
Municipal	19,279	135,531	7
Township	16,656	126,958	8
School district	14,422	88,434	6
Other special district	31,555	84,089	3
Total	**85,006**	**513,200**	**6**

Source: U.S. Bureau of the Census

_____ **23.** Of the following, which is the most common form of local government?

A. municipal
B. township
C. county
D. school district

_____ **24.** The category "other special district" is a type of

A. school district.
B. local government.
C. state government.
D. county government.

_____ **25.** Of the types of local government, which has the greatest total number of elected officials?

A. municipal
B. county
C. school district
D. township

_____ **26.** Which of the following types of local government has the greatest average number of officials?

A. school district
B. municipal
C. township
D. county

_____ **27.** Federal and state governments have a much greater average number of elected officials than local governments. Which of the following best explains this fact?

A. There are more elected officials at the federal and state levels.
B. Local governments are closer to the needs of people.
C. There are more federal and state governments.
D. Federal and state governments represent more people.

Name ______________________ Date __________________ Class ___________

Unit 5 Foundations of Economics

Multiple Choice

Identify the letter of the choice that best completes the statement or answers the question.

_____ **1.** Capital includes

A. soil, minerals, and water.
B. knowledge and skills.
C. tools and factories.
D. time and energy.

_____ **2.** Every society must make all the following basic economic decisions EXCEPT

A. who will get goods and services.
B. how to produce goods and services.
C. what goods and services to produce.
D. how people can share goods and services equally.

_____ **3.** In every society, decisions about who receives goods and services are primarily influenced by

A. historical conflicts.
B. long-term planning.
C. a sense of fairness.
D. society's goals and values.

_____ **4.** The profit motive influences choices most strongly in

A. a command economy.
B. a free market economy.
C. a mixed economy.
D. a traditional economy.

_____ **5.** In a market economy, economic choices are NOT affected by

A. competition.
B. bargaining.
C. central planning.
D. profit seeking.

_____ **6.** Most economic systems of the world today are

A. market economies.
B. command economies.
C. traditional economies.
D. mixed economies.

_____ **7.** A command economy is

A. not based on choices.
B. largely based on choices made by producers and consumers.
C. largely based on choices made by the government.
D. able to meet all the wants of its people.

_____ **8.** The economy of the United States is

A. largely based on choices made by the government.
B. largely based on choices made by producers and consumers.
C. not based on choices.
D. able to meet all the wants of its people.

_____ **9.** Which of the following steps is NOT part of the circular flow of economic activity?

A. Union members strike for higher wages.
B. Producers sell goods for money.
C. Consumers pay money for goods.
D. Individuals work for wages.

_____ **10.** According to the law of demand, when the price of a commodity goes up

A. the supply curve will slope down.
B. the demand curve will slope up.
C. people will usually buy less of it.
D. people will usually buy more of it.

_____ **11.** According to the law of supply, when the price of a good goes up

A. the supply curve will slope down.
B. producers will want to make more of it.
C. producers will want to make less of it.
D. the demand curve will slope up.

_____ **12.** People who start a business take a risk in return for

A. rent, wages, and interest.
B. goods and services.
C. money borrowed from the bank.
D. the hope of earning a profit.

_____ **13.** Entrepreneurs are important in a market economy because they

A. provide interest on investments.
B. keep corporations from getting too large.
C. take risks to start new businesses.
D. make decisions about who should get goods and services.

_____ **14.** The major costs of running a business usually include

A. the market price.
B. shares of stock.
C. profit.
D. wages, rent, and interest.

_____ **15.** Most products, profits, and jobs in the United States are created by

A. sole proprietorships.
B. partnerships.
C. stockholders.
D. corporations.

_____ **16.** American workers formed labor unions because

A. immigrants were taking their jobs.
B. their jobs required special skills.
C. they wanted control over working conditions.
D. they needed work.

_____ **17.** When unions and employers meet to reach agreement on wages and working conditions, it is called

A. strikebreaking.
B. collective bargaining.
C. a sit-down strike.
D. a boycott.

_____ **18.** Labor unions have played a key role in bringing about all of the following gains EXCEPT

A. the shift from a manufacturing to a service economy.
B. banning child labor.
C. minimum wage laws.
D. laws protecting the safety of workers.

_____ **19.** Workers have a basic conflict with employers because

A. Employers want to keep costs high.
B. Workers want to keep profits high.
C. Employers want to increase profits.
D. Workers want to limit wages.

_____ **20.** The first steps in learning how to manage your money include all of the following EXCEPT

A. understanding your income.
B. knowing what your expenses will be.
C. knowing what your goals and values are.
D. understanding stocks.

_____ **21.** Fringe benefits include all of the following EXCEPT

A. sick leave.
B. medical and dental care.
C. paid vacation days.
D. a paycheck.

_____ **22.** Making a budget involves all of the following EXCEPT

A. setting financial goals.
B. not changing a spending plan for at least a year.
C. determining fixed and variable expenses.
D. understanding income.

_____ **23.** In managing your money, you have the most control over

A. your salary.

B. fixed expenses.

C. variable expenses.

D. your rent.

_____ **24.** When deciding whether to purchase an item, you should consider all of the following EXCEPT

A. the price.

B. the ad slogan.

C. the warranty and service.

D. the quality.

_____ **25.** People save money for all of the following reasons EXCEPT

A. to set aside for emergencies.

B. to avoid paying taxes.

C. for large purchases, such as buying a home.

D. to pay for an education or a vacation.

_____ **26.** When deciding which method to use for saving money, you should consider all of the following EXCEPT

A. safety.

B. liquidity.

C. variable expenses.

D. income.

_____ **27.** When deciding on possible careers, you should first think about

A. your interests and abilities.

B. interest rates.

C. insurance plans.

D. where you want to be in 50 years.

ANALYZING LINE GRAPHS

Use the graph below to answer questions 28–30.

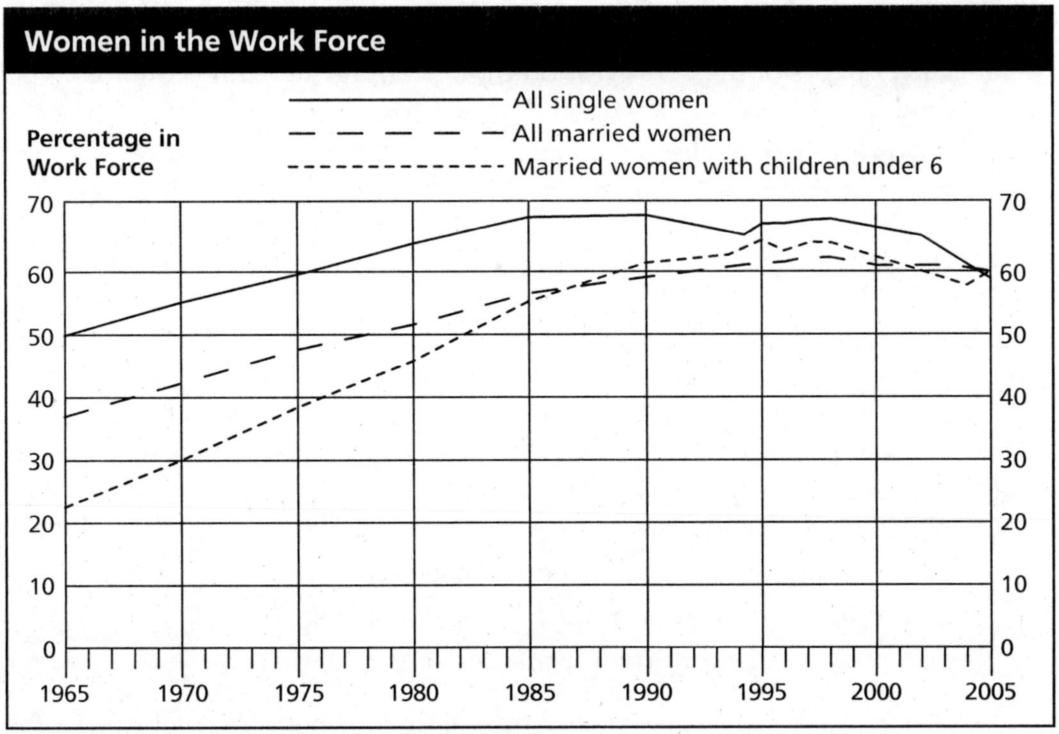

Source: *A Field Guide to the U.S. Economy,* Bureau of Labor Statistics

_____ **28.** In 1965 the percentage of married women who had children under age 6 and who worked outside the home was

A. less than 10 percent.
B. approximately 25 percent.
C. almost 40 percent.
D. about 50 percent.

_____ **29.** More than 50 percent of the women in all the groups shown had entered the work force by

A. 1985.
B. 1970.
C. 1980.
D. 1975.

_____ **30.** During the time period covered by the graph, which group had the largest increase in percentage entering the work force?

A. married women with children under age 6
B. married women without children
C. married women
D. single women

Name ______________________ Date ________________ Class __________

Unit 6 Government and the Economy

Multiple Choice

Identify the letter of the choice that best completes the statement or answers the question.

_____ **1.** The Framers of the Constitution thought the American economy should be a

A. traditional economy.
B. market economy.
C. mixed economy.
D. command economy.

_____ **2.** The government has intervened to attempt to eliminate all of the following EXCEPT

A. dangerous working conditions.
B. damage to the environment.
C. unlimited competition.
D. job discrimination.

_____ **3.** Government affects our economy by taking all the following actions EXCEPT

A. taxing individuals and businesses.
B. limiting the number of people who can hold jobs.
C. controlling the amount of money in the system.
D. making rules for how businesses should operate.

_____ **4.** Which of the following is NOT true of government intervention in the economy?

A. It is always the best solution.
B. It can be controversial.
C. It can limit individual freedom.
D. It can use tax dollars.

_____ **5.** The Sherman and Clayton Acts targeted the practices of

A. monopolies and trusts.
B. farmers.
C. small business owners.
D. teachers.

_____ **6.** Public utilities are examples of legal

A. trusts.
B. public companies.
C. monopolies.
D. corporations.

_____ **7.** A government agency that oversees the safety of items you might buy is the

A. Department of Defense.
B. Food and Drug Administration.
C. Environmental Protection Agency.
D. Federal Trade Commission.

_____ **8.** This series of reforms by President Franklin Roosevelt marked a turning point in the role of government in our economy.

A. Square Deal
B. Great Society
C. New Deal
D. New Frontier

_____ **9.** This government agency investigates cases of pollution.
- **A.** Consumer Product Safety Commission
- **B.** Food and Drug Administration
- **C.** Environmental Protection Agency
- **D.** Federal Trade Commission

_____ **10.** The rate of inflation describes
- **A.** how fast prices are rising.
- **B.** the number of unemployed people who want work.
- **C.** how fast the GDP is going up.
- **D.** the number of people who have jobs.

_____ **11.** As a result of the large national debt, the federal government has to make
- **A.** high interest payments.
- **B.** cuts in revenue.
- **C.** Social Security benefit payments.
- **D.** a budget.

_____ **12.** The three parts of the money supply in the United States are
- **A.** currency, demand deposits, and traveler's checks.
- **B.** checks, bills, and coins.
- **C.** currency, bonds, and traveler's checks.
- **D.** bonds, currency, and demand deposits.

_____ **13.** Money is used in all of the following ways EXCEPT as
- **A.** a measure of the value of goods and services.
- **B.** a means of storing value for the future.
- **C.** a control on gold and silver supplies.
- **D.** a medium of exchange for goods and services.

_____ **14.** In our economy, one characteristic of money is that it
- **A.** is made of highly valued materials.
- **B.** is acceptable to everyone.
- **C.** includes pure silver coins.
- **D.** is easily destroyed.

_____ **15.** United States currency gets its value from
- **A.** the fact that the government says it is money.
- **B.** new discoveries of gold and silver.
- **C.** the value of copper and nickel.
- **D.** the fact that it is easy to carry and use.

_____ **16.** Most of the money supply in the United States is in
- **A.** gold and silver bars.
- **B.** demand deposits.
- **C.** currency.
- **D.** traveler's checks.

_____ **17.** An important role of banks in our economy is
- **A.** making loans.
- **B.** printing money.
- **C.** paying interest on checking accounts.
- **D.** collecting interest on loans.

_____ **18.** Bank loans help the economy grow by helping
- **A.** banks make a profit.
- **B.** people start and expand businesses.
- **C.** people save for personal needs.
- **D.** protect customers' privacy.

_____ **19.** Citizens demanded that government regulate banking because many banks
- **A.** closed and customers lost money.
- **B.** refused to lend money.
- **C.** charged too much interest.
- **D.** stopped growing.

_____ **20.** The Federal Reserve System controls the nation's money supply by
- **A.** making coins and printing new money.
- **B.** influencing the amount of money people borrow.
- **C.** clearing checks and sending them on to the signer's bank.
- **D.** transferring bank funds electronically.

_____ **21.** The Federal Reserve System controls the money supply in order to
- **A.** keep a balance between inflation and recession.
- **B.** encourage inflation and discourage recession.
- **C.** stay out of the normal cycle of inflation and recession.
- **D.** encourage recession and discourage inflation.

_____ **22.** The Employment Act of 1946 stated the government's intention to promote all of the following EXCEPT
- **A.** unemployment.
- **B.** purchasing power.
- **C.** production.
- **D.** employment.

_____ **23.** The process by which our nation keeps track of our overall income and spending is
- **A.** the office of budget management.
- **B.** the office of accounting.
- **C.** certified public accounting.
- **D.** national income accounting.

_____ **24.** The methods of determining income taxes include all of the following EXCEPT

A. progressive tax.
B. regressive tax.
C. proportional tax.
D. sales tax.

_____ **25.** The types of budgets created by governments include all of the following EXCEPT

A. deficit budgets.
B. personal budgets.
C. balanced budgets.
D. surplus budgets.

_____ **26.** The group that helps the President develop his economic policies is the

A. Council of Economic Advisors.
B. Bureau of Budget Affairs.
C. Federal Trade Commission.
D. Equal Employment Opportunity Commission.

_____ **27.** Examples of entitlement programs include all of the following EXCEPT

A. Social Security.
B. Medicare.
C. the Bill of Rights.
D. Medicaid.

Interpreting Graphs

Use the graph below to complete questions 28–31.

Rate of Inflation, 1930–2006

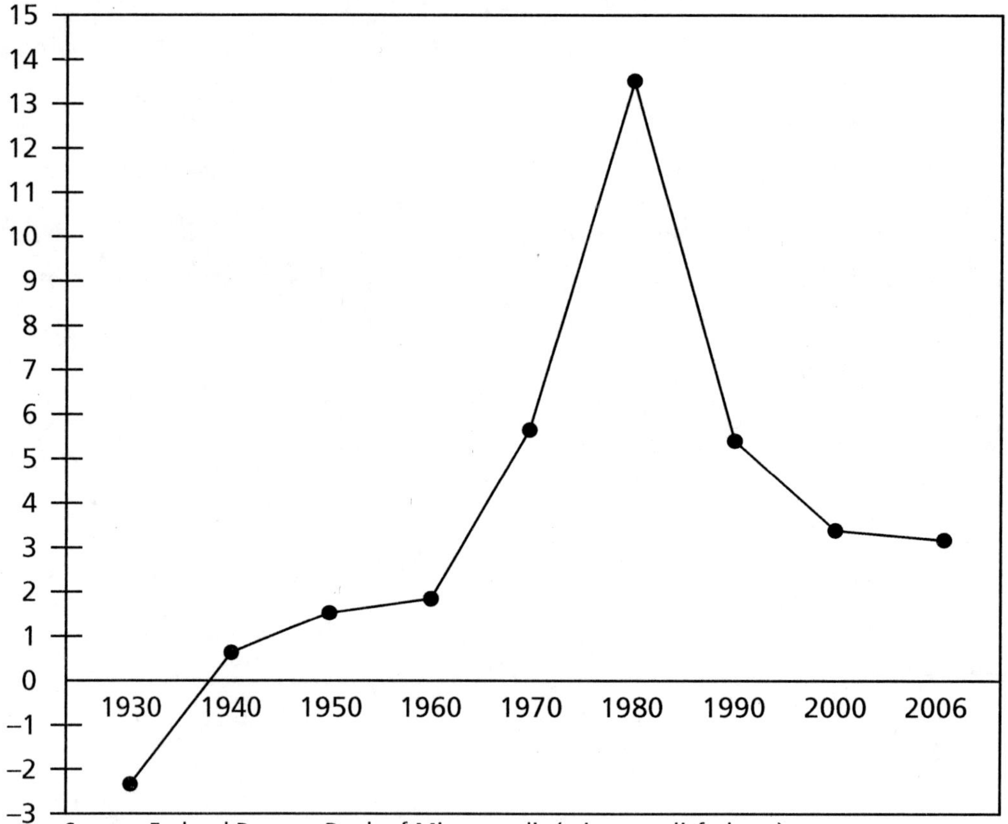

Source: Federal Reserve Bank of Minneapolis (minneapolisfed.org)

_____ **28.** In which years were prices changing at the slowest rate?

A. 1990–2000 **C.** 1980–1990

B. 1970–1980 **D.** 1930–1940

_____ **29.** In which year would the money people earned have bought the fewest goods?

A. 1930 **C.** 1980

B. 1970 **D.** 2000

_____ **30.** What action might the Fed have taken in 1980 to lower the rate of inflation ?

A. lower interest rates **C.** sell government bonds

B. raise interest rates **D.** raise its reserve requirement

_____ **31.** What action might the Fed have taken in 1930 to help the country recover from the Depression?

A. raise the reserve requirement **C.** raise interest rates

B. discourage loans **D.** encourage loans

Name ____________________________ Date ____________________ Class ____________

Unit 7 The American Legal System

Multiple Choice

Identify the letter of the choice that best completes the statement or answers the question.

_____ **1.** One way laws are different from other types of rules is that laws
- **A.** tell people how something should be done.
- **B.** must be obeyed by everyone.
- **C.** identify penalties.
- **D.** set standards.

_____ **2.** Most Americans obey the laws because
- **A.** the laws reflect their morals.
- **B.** they are afraid of the punishments.
- **C.** they do not want to pay fines.
- **D.** they do not want to go to jail.

_____ **3.** A person who takes part in civil disobedience is doing all of the following EXCEPT
- **A.** taking a moral stand.
- **B.** refusing to accept punishment.
- **C.** breaking the law.
- **D.** refusing to obey a law that goes against his or her beliefs.

_____ **4.** Laws passed by Congress usually
- **A.** reflect basic values shared by most Americans.
- **B.** do not have to be obeyed in individual states.
- **C.** apply only in the nation's capital.
- **D.** are called ordinances.

_____ **5.** In deciding a case, judges usually
- **A.** write laws and then apply them.
- **B.** try to make a decision that differs from the decision in a past case.
- **C.** overlook local customs and beliefs.
- **D.** are guided by earlier court decisions.

_____ **6.** One advantage of legal codes is that they
- **A.** do not have to reflect beliefs.
- **B.** are all very ancient.
- **C.** apply only to state laws.
- **D.** organize laws by subject.

_____ **7.** Laws are sometimes changed because
A. they can be organized into a legal code.
B. they follow precedents.
C. government agencies disagree with the legislature.
D. people's beliefs and values change.

_____ **8.** An action is not a crime until
A. it hurts other people.
B. the person who does it is arrested.
C. a law is written against it.
D. lots of people start doing it.

_____ **9.** In a criminal case, the main question is
A. "What is a fair way to settle this disagreement?"
B. "What should this person's fine be?"
C. "Did this person commit this crime?"
D. "For how long should this person go to jail?"

_____ **10.** In a civil case, the main question is
A. "What should this person's fine be?"
B. "What is a fair way to settle this disagreement?"
C. "For how long should this person go to jail?"
D. "Did this person commit this crime?"

_____ **11.** Which statement is NOT true of crime in the United States?
A. Wealthy neighborhoods have more crime than poor ones.
B. Crime costs people billions of dollars each year.
C. Americans view crime as one of the most important problems in the country.
D. A crime of some type is committed every **3** seconds.

_____ **12.** A planned killing is called
A. assault.
B. manslaughter.
C. murder.
D. self-defense.

_____ **13.** The most frequent type of crime is
A. white-collar crime.
B. crime against people.
C. crime against property.
D. crime against the government.

_____ **14.** One act that is a crime against both a person and property is
A. burglary.
B. robbery.
C. larceny.
D. embezzlement.

_____ **15.** Victimless crimes are considered crimes for all the following reasons EXCEPT they

A. keep the police force busy.

B. may hurt the people who commit them.

C. hurt society as a whole.

D. go against the common values of the country.

_____ **16.** People blame all the following conditions for crime EXCEPT

A. harsh courts.

B. television violence.

C. poverty.

D. drug abuse.

_____ **17.** In order to find a defendant guilty in a criminal trial, a jury must

A. first decide the sentence.

B. have no important doubts.

C. question witnesses.

D. make closing arguments.

_____ **18.** All of the following are problems of our criminal justice system EXCEPT

A. too many cases and too few judges.

B. the success of rehabilitation programs.

C. overcrowded prisons.

D. public doubts about whether the system works.

_____ **19.** The main goal of the juvenile justice system is to

A. help, not punish, juveniles.

B. hear cases in criminal courts.

C. build special jails for juvenile delinquents.

D. place young people on probation.

_____ **20.** Juvenile court hearings differ from adult court trials in that

A. the defendant has no right to a jury trial.

B. the judge decides on a sentence.

C. the prosecutor presents the facts of the case.

D. the defense attorney questions witnesses.

_____ **21.** Civil cases are settled according to the principles of

A. fines and equity.

B. damages and injunctions.

C. punishment and lawsuits.

D. compensation and equity.

_____ **22.** Civil cases may involve any of the following issues EXCEPT

A. broken contracts.

B. divorce.

C. personal injury.

D. misdemeanors.

_____ **23.** One goal of all civil cases is to
- **A.** issue an injunction.
- **B.** make sure that the defendant pays damages to the plaintiff.
- **C.** sentence the guilty person to a prison term.
- **D.** place responsibility where it belongs.

_____ **24.** A civil lawsuit begins when
- **A.** a jury is called to hear evidence.
- **B.** the plaintiff files an answer.
- **C.** the defendant posts bail.
- **D.** the plaintiff files a complaint.

_____ **25.** Which statement describes a way in which civil cases differ from criminal cases?
- **A.** Evidence is presented.
- **B.** Witnesses are questioned.
- **C.** A judge keeps order.
- **D.** The verdict is based on a preponderance of evidence.

_____ **26.** Which is NOT a reason that civil cases often take a long time?
- **A.** Collecting evidence takes time.
- **B.** Court rules permit lawyers to delay trials.
- **C.** Plaintiffs often drop cases they cannot win.
- **D.** There are not enough judges and courtrooms.

_____ **27.** A "mock trial" can be described as
- **A.** an arbitration.
- **B.** a preview of a jury trial.
- **C.** a rent-a-judge trial.
- **D.** a mediation.

_____ **28.** One reason people take cases to small claims court is that it
- **A.** takes little time.
- **B.** does not allow witnesses.
- **C.** awards higher damages.
- **D.** uses a smaller jury.

_____ **29.** Storefront legal offices usually
- **A.** do not have qualified attorneys.
- **B.** cost more in the end than other types of legal offices.
- **C.** cheat people.
- **D.** offer set prices for certain legal services.

_____ **30.** As a result of large damage awards in civil lawsuits,
- **A.** the cost of insurance has dropped.
- **B.** juries are no longer used in personal injury cases.
- **C.** everyone who suffers serious loss is paid fairly.
- **D.** some cities no longer provide some services.

Analyzing Statistical Tables

Use the table below to choose the letter of the best answer.

Typical Lengths of Parts of Some Criminal Jury Trials* (in hours and minutes)

	Narcotics	Assault	Robbery	Homicide
Jury Selection	2:00	2:11	3:00	8:14
Prosecutor's Case	2:49	4:06	3:41	13:43
Defense Case	1:30	1:47	1:40	4:38
Jury Deliberation	2:12	2:38	1:50	5:30

*Based on data gathered from over 1,500 trials in New Jersey and California
Source: *On Trial: The Length of Civil and Criminal Trials.* Williamsburg National Center for State Courts

_____ **31.** In which type of trial does the selection of the jury usually take the least time?

A. robbery
B. homicide
C. narcotics
D. assault

_____ **32.** The type of trial that takes the longest time overall usually involves

A. narcotics.
B. homicide.
C. assault.
D. robbery.

_____ **33.** The side that takes the longest to present its case is the side that wants to show

A. the innocence of the defendant.
B. the guilt of the defendant.
C. the guilt of the plaintiff.
D. the innocence of the plaintiff.

_____ **34.** From the data, you can conclude ONLY that, typically,

A. homicide trials generally take longer than other trials.
B. there are twice as many narcotics trials as assault trials.
C. narcotics cases are not as important as robbery cases.
D. defense attorneys do not try very hard in narcotics cases.

_____ **35.** Of the crimes listed on this particular table, you might conclude that the one a jury is likely to judge most carefully is

A. robbery.
B. assault.
C. homicide.
D. narcotics.

Name ______________________ Date ________________ Class __________

Unit 8 People Make a Difference

Multiple Choice

Identify the letter of the choice that best completes the statement or answers the question.

_____ 1. Nonpartisan offices are ones for which
- A. parties take turns electing candidates.
- B. candidates do not declare themselves to be members of parties.
- C. the person who is elected may not belong to a party.
- D. parties work together to set goals.

_____ 2. All of the following are roles of political parties EXCEPT
- A. saving citizens the trouble of voting.
- B. nominating candidates for office.
- C. serving as government watchdogs.
- D. providing day-to-day leadership in government.

_____ 3. Political parties help all Americans by
- A. fund-raising.
- B. patronage.
- C. running elections.
- D. informing them about issues.

_____ 4. The first political parties
- A. still exist today.
- B. were established by the Constitution.
- C. formed to elect George Washington.
- D. arose because of differing views of the role of government.

_____ 5. Third parties
- A. do not last beyond one election.
- B. were established by the Constitution.
- C. can influence the ideas of major parties.
- D. often succeed in electing a President.

_____ 6. Today's Democratic Party was first lead by
- A. George Wahsington
- B. Franklin Roosevelt
- C. Thomas Jefferson
- D. Andrew Jackson

_____ **7.** The Democratic and Republican parties disagree most strongly about

A. basic American beliefs.

B. what the role of the federal government should be.

C. whether or not to take extreme stands on issues.

D. how a party should be organized.

_____ **8.** Party strength seems to be declining for all of the following reasons EXCEPT

A. changes in patronage.

B. a greater number of independent voters.

C. the growing independence of candidates.

D. an increase in straight-ticket voting.

_____ **9.** In a closed primary, a voter must

A. be registered as a party member.

B. pay a fee before voting.

C. not be running for office.

D. have contributed to the candidate's campaign.

_____ **10.** One example of patronage today is

A. the civil service system.

B. the President's Cabinet.

C. a political party.

D. Congress.

_____ **11.** Most candidates for state and federal office are chosen by

A. national convention.

B. caucus.

C. direct primary.

D. self-nomination.

_____ **12.** Limits on individual contributions to presidential candidates have been set by

A. party platforms.

B. tradition.

C. federal laws.

D. nominating conventions.

_____ **13.** One major role of a party's national convention is to

A. nominate candidates for Congress.

B. approve the party platform.

C. organize the state caucuses.

D. choose delegates.

_____ **14.** General elections

A. fill federal, state, and local offices.

B. include only ballot measures.

C. fill only federal offices.

D. are held to choose candidates for President.

_____ **15.** In most states voters must be all of the following EXCEPT

A. registered.

B. employed.

C. at least 18 years old.

D. a resident of the state in which they vote.

_____ **16.** Which of the following is NOT true of elections?

A. If you cannot get to the polling place, you may not vote.

B. Primary and local elections may take place at any time during the year.

C. Special elections may be held at any time.

D. Federal elections take place in November.

_____ **17.** Which of the following voting methods is NOT currently used in modern elections?

A. paper ballot

B. show of hands

C. punch cards

D. electronic touchpads

_____ **18.** One type of ballot that proved controversial in the 2000 presidential election was the

A. caterpillar ballot

B. accordian ballot

C. butterfly ballot

D. paper ballot

_____ **19.** People give all of the following reasons for voting EXCEPT

A. they believe that every vote counts.

B. they want to support candidates who best represent them.

C. they think that all the candidates are the same.

D. they want to try to change government policies.

_____ **20.** Which of the following is generally the BEST source of information on a candidate?

A. direct mail

B. debates between candidates

C. posters and bumper stickers

D. television ads

_____ **21.** Political action committees (PACs)

A. give large sums of money to election campaigns.

B. are funded by political parties.

C. have been banned.

D. have tried to get rid of interest groups.

_____ **22.** Propaganda is
- **A.** gathering political opinions.
- **B.** a message meant to influence ideas or actions.
- **C.** lies and false information.
- **D.** straight talk about issues.

_____ **23.** Critics of television coverage of campaigns claim that TV
- **A.** makes election issues seem unimportant.
- **B.** does not cover the exciting activities of candidates.
- **C.** should use "sound-bites."
- **D.** gives the public too much information.

Analyzing Bar Graphs

Use the graphs below to choose the letter of the best answer.

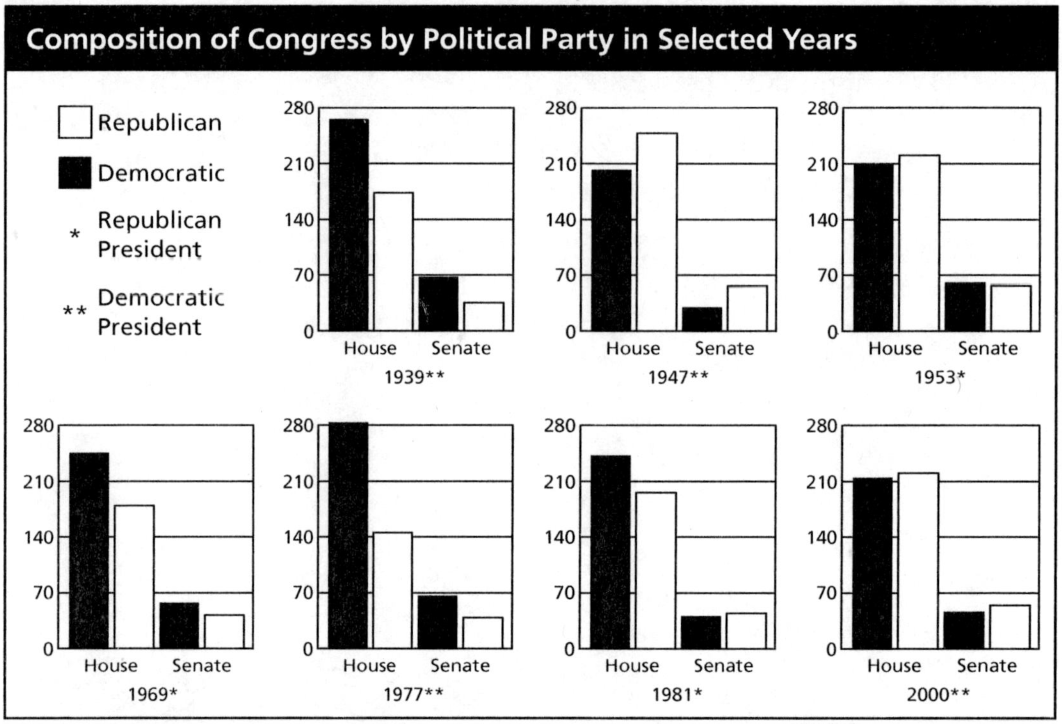

Source: *Statistical Abstract of the United States*

_____ **24.** The number of Democrats in the House of Representatives was greatest in the year

A. 1977.
B. 1939.
C. 2000.
D. 1947.

_____ **25.** In what year did one party have a majority in the House but a minority in the Senate?

A. 1981
B. 1953
C. 1947
D. 1977

_____ **26.** In **2000** the President and the majority of members of Congress were, respectively,

A. a Republican and Democrats.
B. a Republican and Republicans.
C. a Democrat and Democrats.
D. a Democrat and Republicans.

_____ **27.** In which years do you think Congress was most likely to pass laws supporting the President's policies?

A. 1981 and 1995
B. 1947 and 1977
C. 1939 and 1947
D. 1939 and 1977

Name ______________________ Date __________________ Class ___________

Unit 9 The United States and the World

Multiple Choice

Identify the letter of the choice that best completes the statement or answers the question.

_____ **1.** All of the following are basic characteristics of a nation EXCEPT

A. having territory with borders.
B. having sovereignty.
C. having a government.
D. having colonies.

_____ **2.** Which nation is thousands of years old?

A. Andorra
B. Rwanda
C. Australia
D. China

_____ **3.** Which of the following is NOT a reason that a colonial power would establish a colony?

A. to gain new lands for settlers
B. to gain a source of cheap labor
C. to use the natural resources of the area
D. to improve the standard of living of the native peoples

_____ **4.** Developed and developing nations differ mainly in that

A. developing nations are all industrialized.
B. there is no poverty in developed nations.
C. their standards of living differ.
D. developed nations all used to be colonies.

_____ **5.** The arms race between the United States and the Soviet Union was an example of international

A. détente.
B. cooperation.
C. competition.
D. interdependence.

_____ **6.** NATO is an example of

A. a national organization.
B. an alliance.
C. a federal government.
D. an economic community.

_____ **7.** One result of détente between the two superpowers was

A. the Cold War.
B. the Korean War.
C. the INF Treaty.
D. the formation of the European Community.

_____ **8.** Which of the following is NOT a cause of interdependence among nations?
- **A.** environmental problems
- **B.** feelings of nationalism
- **C.** improved communication
- **D.** world trade

_____ **9.** The existence of multinational corporations is evidence of
- **A.** the cold war.
- **B.** a global economy.
- **C.** concerns about the environment.
- **D.** the rise of nationalism.

_____ **10.** The most important characteristic of the world as a system is that
- **A.** a change in one part will affect the other parts.
- **B.** the whole is less important than the parts.
- **C.** it relies on technology.
- **D.** the parts can operate independently.

_____ **11.** All of the following are goals of American foreign policy EXCEPT
- **A.** encouraging respect for human rights.
- **B.** decreasing foreign trade.
- **C.** ensuring national security.
- **D.** maintaining peace.

_____ **12.** All of the following are tools of American foreign policy EXCEPT
- **A.** democracy.
- **B.** diplomacy.
- **C.** alliances.
- **D.** defense.

_____ **13.** The relations and communications carried out between countries are known as
- **A.** foreign aid.
- **B.** diplomacy.
- **C.** summit meetings.
- **D.** trade measures.

_____ **14.** American foreign aid can help our government meet its goals in all of the following ways EXCEPT
- **A.** rebuilding American industries.
- **B.** developing trading partners.
- **C.** reducing the chances of revolution and war.
- **D.** helping other countries defend against aggression.

_____ **15.** The Department of State plays an important role in foreign policy by
- **A.** resisting diplomatic immunity.
- **B.** approving treaties.
- **C.** its power to declare war.
- **D.** carrying out the President's policies.

_____ **16.** In terms of foreign policy, American labor groups would most likely recommend

A. limiting exports.

B. increasing imports.

C. taxing imports.

D. building factories in developing countries.

_____ **17.** Mikhail Gorbachev's policies of openness in the Soviet Union had the effect of

A. increasing tensions between the Soviet Union and the United States.

B. tightening government control over the Soviet people.

C. reducing trade between the Soviet Union and the United States.

D. easing tensions between the Soviet Union and the United States.

_____ **18.** American policy toward the Middle East has been greatly affected by

A. European economic power.

B. Middle East production of manufactured goods.

C. conflict between Arabs and Israelis.

D. lack of support for Israel.

_____ **19.** Which of the following is NOT a danger of the arms race?

A. biological weapons

B. nerve gas

C. CFCs

D. nuclear missiles

_____ **20.** Terrorism is

A. an attempt to end human rights violations.

B. a protest against technology.

C. the use or threat of violence to reach political goals.

D. confined to Middle Eastern countries.

_____ **21.** All of the following are goals of the United Nations EXCEPT

A. promote justice.

B. become a "super-government."

C. preserve world peace.

D. encourage international cooperation.

_____ **22.** The UN General Assembly does NOT

A. discuss global problems.

B. pave the way for international agreements.

C. make laws.

D. decide how the UN will spend its money.

_____ **23.** World Court judges

A. work with international law.

B. make the decisions that are binding to all nations.

C. oversee the actions of the UN.

D. have to come to a unanimous decision.

_____ **24.** One UN committee that was so successful in fulfilling its original goals that it is now suspended is the

A. Trusteeship Council.

B. Economic and Social Council.

C. Security Council.

D. World Court.

_____ **25.** A private group whose main goal is to aid victims of war is

A. the Ford Foundation.

B. Doctors Without Borders.

C. Amnesty International.

D. Greenpeace.

ANALYZING STATISTICAL TABLES

Use the table below to choose the letter of the best answer.

Top Ten Foreign Countries Receiving the Most United States Aid, 2007

Country	Amount of Aid
Iraq	$6,926,000,000
Afghanistan	1,060,000,000
Egypt	750,000,000
Sudan	575,000,000
Ethiopia	552,000,000
Jordan	368,000,000
Colombia	366,000,000
Palestinian Adm. Areas	227,000,000
Uganda	255,000,000
Pakistan	224,000,000

Source: Global issues.org

_____ **26.** From the table you can learn which of the following?

A. the reason aid was needed
B. the amount of aid given
C. the nation's form of government
D. the population of the nation

_____ **27.** In 2007, Ethiopia received more United States aid than

A. Uganda.
B. Sudan.
C. Egypt.
D. Iraq.

_____ **28.** The amount of aid received by Afghanistan was about five times the amount received by

A. Jordan.
B. Colombia.
C. Pakistan.
D. Uganda.

_____ **29.** The region to which the United States gave the most aid in 2007 could be labeled

A. Western Europe.
B. Southeast Asia.
C. Africa.
D. the Middle East.

_____ **30.** Which of the following could be inferred from the table?

A. The United States gave most of its military aid to African nations.
B. Most aid is in the form of famine relief.
C. The Middle East is a key area in American foreign policy.
D. The United States is most concerned with Western Europe.

Name ______________________ Date ________________ Class __________

First-Semester Exam

Multiple Choice

Identify the letter of the choice that best completes the statement or answers the question.

_____ **1.** The "American cultural mosaic" refers to

A. works of many different artists.
B. immigrants who have given up their native heritage.
C. elements of many cultures that have combined to make up American culture.
D. the early settlers of our nation.

_____ **2.** The second largest population group in the United States is

A. Asian Americans.
B. Native Americans.
C. African Americans.
D. European Americans.

_____ **3.** In the United States, diversity includes all of the following EXCEPT

A. coming from different backgrounds.
B. thinking of ourselves as Americans.
C. being different ages.
D. speaking different languages.

_____ **4.** All of the following are true about discrimination EXCEPT

A. it is unfair.
B. it denies equal opportunities to people.
C. it is a result of racism.
D. it no longer occurs in the United States.

_____ **5.** American citizens do NOT have the right to

A. criticize the government.
B. practice discrimination.
C. a fair trial.
D. vote.

_____ **6.** Justice in the United States means that people should

A. be treated exactly the same as all other people.
B. make the same salary for the same job.
C. be treated fairly.
D. be able to say and do what they want.

_____ **7.** The basic American value of justice can also be called

A. liberty.
B. equality.
C. fairness.
D. discrimination.

_____ **8.** The basic American value of equality means that

A. anyone can hold elective office.

B. racism does not exist.

C. everyone is equally good at things.

D. everyone should have the same rights and opportunities.

_____ **9.** Which of the following are values?

A. equality, ideals, beliefs

B. diversity, beliefs, equality

C. freedom, diversity, ideals

D. equality, freedom, justice

_____ **10.** Rules are

A. the same thing as values.

B. general standards that guide our behavior.

C. based on values.

D. not a part of social groups.

_____ **11.** Learning how to be a member of a group is called

A. social interaction.

B. socialization.

C. society.

D. socializing.

_____ **12.** The most basic institution in any society is the

A. family.

B. government.

C. school.

D. church.

_____ **13.** The institution of education is important to society for all of the following reasons EXCEPT

A. it helps people meet others with different values.

B. it helps people reach their dreams and goals.

C. it satisfies people's wants and needs for goods and services.

D. it teaches the beliefs and values that hold us together as a society.

_____ **14.** All of the following are American economic freedoms EXCEPT

A. the freedom to choose an occupation.

B. the freedom to buy and sell.

C. the freedom to own property.

D. the freedom to not be a consumer.

_____ **15.** Each of us is a consumer because we

A. provide skills and labor to produce goods.

B. live in a democracy.

C. purchase goods and services.

D. use the barter system rather than money.

_____ **16.** Contributing to the common good does NOT include
  A. voting.
  B. littering.
  C. recycling soda cans.
  D. visiting patients in a nursing home.

_____ **17.** You are an American citizen if any of the following is true EXCEPT
  A. you were born in another country and were over 18 years old when your parents were naturalized.
  B. you have been naturalized.
  C. at least one of your parents was a United States citizen when you were born.
  D. you were born in the United States.

_____ **18.** Your rights as a citizen include
  A. the right to refuse to serve on a jury.
  B. the right to say what you think in writing.
  C. the right to use your personal property any way you want.
  D. unlimited freedom.

_____ **19.** A citizen of the United States must
  A. defend the nation.
  B. be a church member.
  C. join important civic clubs.
  D. read the newspaper.

_____ **20.** Trying to influence the government is
  A. one of the duties of a citizen.
  B. against the law.
  C. usually not possible.
  D. not a very good idea for the average citizen.

_____ **21.** Our system of government is called a
  A. monarchy.
  B. democracy.
  C. dictatorship.
  D. constitutional monarchy.

_____ **22.** An unjust use of government power is called a
  A. tyranny.
  B. parliament.
  C. republic.
  D. monarchy.

_____ **23.** The ideas of direct democracy came to the colonists from
  A. the Magna Carta.
  B. the Framers.
  C. ancient Athens.
  D. the Roman republic.

_____ **24.** In the colonies the right to vote was held by

A. anyone who could read and write.

B. white men who owned a certain amount of land.

C. men and women over the age of 21.

D. all men.

_____ **25.** The best example of a direct democracy would be

A. the House of Representatives voting on a bill.

B. the Senate voting on a treaty.

C. the student council meeting to choose school colors.

D. the students in a classroom voting on party refreshments.

_____ **26.** The Articles of Confederation needed to be revised for all of the following reasons EXCEPT that the Congress

A. needed more power to deal with other nations.

B. could not raise enough money for the government.

C. agreed on what new form of government was needed.

D. could not enforce the laws.

_____ **27.** Which of the following statements accurately describes the Magna Carta?

A. The Magna Carta was the charter of Roman republic.

B. The Magna Carta listed rights that the English monarch could not take away.

C. The Magna Carta guaranteed freedom of the press.

D. The Magna Carta granted the colonies their independence.

_____ **28.** "Checks and balances" means that

A. each branch of the government has ways to limit the power of the other branches.

B. each side gives up part of what it wants.

C. the legislative branch is divided into two houses.

D. the country has a strong federal government.

_____ **29.** When we call the United States a marketplace of ideas, we mean that

A. the press, radio, and television are not limited in any way.

B. the government may not establish a religion.

C. all views, even unpopular ones, may be expressed.

D. we are all consumers.

_____ **30.** One reason the Constitution has endured for more than 200 years is that

A. people have always agreed about what it means.

B. it contains only general principles, which can be interpreted.

C. the Framers set down every detail for how the government should be run.

D. it cannot be changed.

_____ **31.** Federalism is the principle of

A. division of power between the state and national governments.

B. giving each branch of government ways to limit the power of the other branches.

C. checks and balances.

D. separation of powers within the federal government.

_____ **32.** The main argument for adding the Bill of Rights was that it would

A. make more people vote in favor of the Constitution.

B. give the new government more power to free the country from England.

C. make the Constitution more like the English Constitution.

D. gain support for the new government.

_____ **33.** The main argument against the Bill of Rights was that it

A. was unpopular with the people and would cause the Constitution to be defeated.

B. limited the power of the people too much.

C. was not needed.

D. was unconstitutional.

_____ **34.** Your right to get a group of people together to ask the government to change a law is protected by

A. the Fifth Amendment.

B. the First Amendment.

C. the Fourth Amendment.

D. the Sixth Amendment.

_____ **35.** The amendment that gave African American men the right to vote was the

A. Twenty-fourth.

B. Fifteenth.

C. Thirteenth.

D. Fourteenth.

_____ **36.** The group that gained the right to vote most recently is

A. men and women between the ages of 18 and 21.

B. African Americans.

C. immigrants.

D. women.

_____ **37.** The decision in *Brown* v. *Board of Education of Topeka* called for
A. equal protection under the law.
B. affirmative action.
C. the separate but equal doctrine.
D. segregation.

_____ **38.** The Supreme Court decision that made it unconstitutional to have separate hiring policies for men and women was
A. *Brown* v. *Board of Education of Topeka.*
B. *Plessy* v. *Ferguson.*
C. *Regents of the University of California* v. *Bakke.*
D. *Phillips* v. *Martin Marietta Corporation.*

_____ **39.** Affirmative action means
A. schools that separate races cannot be equal.
B. women and minorities should be encouraged to vote.
C. universities should not discriminate against women and minorities.
D. employers should make an effort to hire women and minorities.

_____ **40.** A member of Congress is responsible to
A. the whole nation.
B. his or her political party.
C. constituents.
D. all of the above.

_____ **41.** The total number of representatives in the House of Representatives
A. depends on the number of congressional districts.
B. is set by state legislatures.
C. changes after every census.
D. is 435.

_____ **42.** The two Senators from a state each
A. are appointed by their political party.
B. serve two-year terms.
C. represent one half of the state.
D. represent the entire state.

_____ **43.** Congress does NOT have the power to
A. spend money.
B. declare war.
C. create federal courts.
D. appoint ambassadors.

_____ **44.** Leaders in the House and Senate are chosen by
A. the President.
B. a conference committee.
C. both the Democratic and Republican parties.
D. the majority party.

_____ **45.** Congressional committees do all of the following EXCEPT
- **A.** recommend bills for a vote in the House or Senate.
- **B.** send bills to the President to sign.
- **C.** conduct investigations.
- **D.** study and hold public hearings on bills.

_____ **46.** In order to become a law, a bill must be
- **A.** passed by both houses of Congress.
- **B.** vetoed by the President.
- **C.** approved by both political parties.
- **D.** approved by the Supreme Court.

_____ **47.** All of the following are powers of Congress EXCEPT
- **A.** collecting taxes.
- **B.** regulating trade between states.
- **C.** declaring war.
- **D.** appointing federal judges.

_____ **48.** The Speaker of the House is chosen by
- **A.** the President.
- **B.** the president pro tempore.
- **C.** the majority party in the House.
- **D.** the floor leaders in Congress.

_____ **49.** The President's most important job is to
- **A.** set national goals and develop foreign and domestic policies.
- **B.** represent the voters.
- **C.** make laws.
- **D.** direct the bureaucracy.

_____ **50.** The State of the Union message is an example of the President's role as
- **A.** chief diplomat.
- **B.** chief executive.
- **C.** legislative leader.
- **D.** party leader.

_____ **51.** The President can carry out policies in all the following ways EXCEPT by
- **A.** giving executive orders.
- **B.** making executive agreements.
- **C.** making laws.
- **D.** appointing Supreme Court justices.

_____ **52.** Heads of executive departments include all of the following EXCEPT
- **A.** the Secretary of the Treasury.
- **B.** the Attorney General.
- **C.** the National Security Advisor.
- **D.** the Secretary of Defense.

_____ **53.** "Executive privilege" means that the President

A. gets to entertain visiting foreign leaders.
B. may make trade agreements without approval by Congress.
C. must be obeyed by members of the bureaucracy.
D. may keep some information secret from Congress and the courts.

_____ **54.** Which of the following is NOT a limit on the President's power?

A. term of office
B. executive orders
C. checks and balances
D. separation of powers

_____ **55.** All of the following are powers of the executive branch EXCEPT

A. pardoning someone convicted of a crime.
B. making sure laws are carried out.
C. amending the Constitution.
D. vetoing legislation.

_____ **56.** The role of the Vice President is largely determined by

A. Congress.
B. voters.
C. the President.
D. the Constitution.

_____ **57.** The defendant in a trial is

A. on the same side as the prosecution.
B. the person against whom a complaint is brought.
C. also known as the plaintiff.
D. usually not known at the beginning of a trial.

_____ **58.** The Supreme Court uses its power of judicial review when it

A. hears cases involving disputes between state governments.
B. chooses which appeals cases to hear.
C. follows precedent.
D. rules that a law is unconstitutional.

_____ **59.** Checks on the judicial branch include all of the following EXCEPT

A. the Senate's power to confirm judicial appointments.
B. the President's power to remove justices.
C. the power of Congress to propose constitutional amendments.
D. the President's power to appoint judges.

_____ **60.** Courts do all of the following EXCEPT

A. apply the law to an actual situation.
B. decide if the Constitution is reasonable.
C. decide whether a person is innocent or guilty.
D. decide what the punishment will be.

_____ **61.** The Supreme Court's decision in the *Marbury* v. *Madison* case established the precedent of

A. judicial restraint.
B. judicial decision-making.
C. judicial activism.
D. judicial review.

_____ **62.** The system of dividing power between the state and federal governments is called

A. checks and balances.
B. federalism.
C. a more perfect union.
D. separation of powers.

_____ **63.** State governments have the power

A. to set up public schools.
B. to declare war.
C. to coin money.
D. to make treaties with other countries.

_____ **64.** Those who argue for a strong federal government say that, compared with state governments, it is

A. closer to the needs of citizens.
B. more willing to experiment.
C. better at providing equality.
D. more flexible.

_____ **65.** Seats in the upper houses of state legislatures are apportioned on the basis of

A. number of people.
B. tradition.
C. number of voters.
D. geographic area.

_____ **66.** The executive branch of state government is headed by

A. the assembly.
B. the Supreme Court.
C. the Cabinet.
D. the governor.

_____ **67.** Governors usually have the most control over the

A. other top executive branch officials.
B. legislature.
C. state constitution.
D. budget.

_____ **68.** All of the following are powers of the states EXCEPT the power to

A. coin money.
B. set up local governments.
C. set up public school systems.
D. conduct elections.

_____ **69.** A process by which voters can propose laws is known as
A. recall.
B. referendum.
C. impeachment.
D. initiative.

_____ **70.** All of the following are powers of a governor EXCEPT
A. making sure laws are enforced.
B. approving the state budget.
C. item veto power.
D. pardoning criminals.

_____ **71.** All of the following are methods of selecting state judges EXCEPT
A. the Missouri Plan.
B. appointment by the governor.
C. election.
D. appointment by the President.

_____ **72.** Local governments get their power from
A. Congress.
B. state governments.
C. the U.S. Constitution.
D. county boards.

_____ **73.** The plan in which a city council acts as both a legislative and executive body is known as the
A. commission plan.
B. council-manager plan.
C. weak-mayor plan.
D. strong-mayor plan.

_____ **74.** Counties are usually governed by
A. a county clerk.
B. a mayor and council.
C. an elected board.
D. a sheriff.

_____ **75.** The plan for local government that most closely resembles the federal government is called the
A. commission plan.
B. council-manager plan.
C. home rule plan.
D. mayor-council plan.

_____ **76.** Intergovernmental revenue is money that
A. local governments give to each other.
B. state and federal governments give to local government.
C. local governments pay to the state.
D. local governments pay to the federal government.

_____ **77.** The major point of conflict between local, state, and federal governments is
A. how to use land.
B. how to control pollution.
C. how to slow business growth.
D. how to spend grant money.

Using Primary Sources

Use the excerpts from the Declaration of Independence below to choose the letter of the best answer.

Excerpt 1

We hold these truths to be self-evident, that all men are created equal, that they are endowed by their Creator with certain unalienable rights, that among these are life, liberty, and the pursuit of happiness. That, to secure these rights, governments are instituted among men, deriving their just powers from the consent of the governed. That, whenever any form of government becomes destructive of these ends, it is the right of the people to alter or to abolish it. . . .

Excerpt 2

Prudence, indeed, will dictate that governments long established should not be changed for light and transient causes; and, accordingly, all experience has shown that mankind are more disposed to suffer, while evils are sufferable, than to right themselves by abolishing the forms to which they are accustomed.

Excerpt 3

But when a long train of abuses and "usurpations . . . evinces" a design to reduce them under absolute despotism, it is their right, it is their duty, to throw off such government, and to provide new guards for their future security.

Excerpt 4

We, therefore, the representatives of the United States of America, in General Congress assembled, appealing to the Supreme Judge of the world for the rectitude of our intentions, do, in the name and by authority of the good people of these colonies, solemnly publish and declare, that these united colonies are and of right ought to be free and independent states; that they are absolved from all allegiance to the British Crown, and that all political connection between them and the state of Great Britain is and ought to be totally dissolved.

_____ **78.** Excerpt 1 says that governments are

A. given their power by the agreement of the people.
B. the possessors of certain rights that cannot be taken away.
C. generally destructive.
D. created by God to protect people's rights.

_____ **79.** Excerpt 2 says that people

A. want to get rid of slavery.
B. should change their government whenever they wish.
C. will put up with a lot before they try to change government.
D. usually want new governments.

_____ **80.** Excerpt 3 says that

A. kings should be eliminated.
B. people have a duty to create good governments.
C. people need security forces.
D. any government would be better than the British government.

_____ **81.** Excerpt 4 says that the Declaration of Independence was written by

A. representatives of the people of the colonies.

B. the Congress.

C. the Supreme Court.

D. all the people of the colonies.

_____ **82.** Excerpt 4 says that the people of the United States

A. will create a new monarchy.

B. declare their independence.

C. intend to go to war against Great Britain to gain independence.

D. ally themselves with Great Britain.

Interpreting Maps

Use the map below to answer the questions that follow.

Congressional Apportionment, 2003–2013

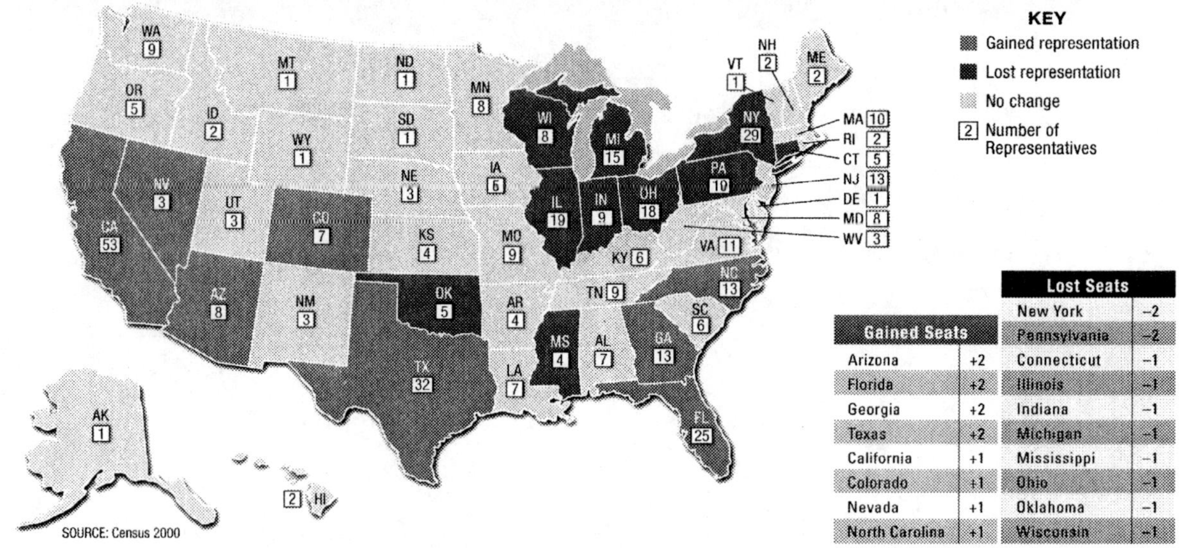

Gained Seats	
Arizona	+2
Florida	+2
Georgia	+2
Texas	+2
California	+1
Colorado	+1
Nevada	+1
North Carolina	+1

Lost Seats	
New York	–2
Pennsylvania	–2
Connecticut	–1
Illinois	–1
Indiana	–1
Michigan	–1
Mississippi	–1
Ohio	–1
Oklahoma	–1
Wisconsin	–1

_____ **83.** The map shows

A. the number of people who live in each state.
B. the total population of the United States.
C. changes in House representation.
D. the location of House districts in the states.

_____ **84.** Which statement about the map is NOT true?

A. Some states gained seats in the House of Representatives.
B. Some states lost seats in the House of Representatives.
C. The total number of seats in the House of Representatives increased.
D. Some states kept the same number of seats in the House of Representatives.

Name ____________________ Date ______________ Class __________

Second-Semester Exam

Multiple Choice

Identify the letter of the choice that best completes the statement or answers the question.

_____ **1.** All of the following are true about the factors of production EXCEPT
  A. people use them to produce goods and services.
  B. people use them to satisfy wants.
  C. they include land, labor, and capital.
  D. they are unlimited.

_____ **2.** The three basic resources for producing goods and services are
  A. food, clothing, and shelter.
  B. production, distribution, and consumption.
  C. labor, land, and capital.
  D. wants, needs, and choices.

_____ **3.** Over time, people's economic wants and needs are
  A. mainly for food, clothing, and shelter.
  B. the same in every country.
  C. easily satisfied.
  D. greater than the resources available to satisfy them.

_____ **4.** In every economic system, all of the following are basic economic decisions EXCEPT
  A. what goods and services to produce.
  B. who will get goods and services.
  C. how to produce goods and services.
  D. what goals and values individuals should have.

_____ **5.** An economic system is a way for a society to
  A. make profits from investments.
  B. train workers for future jobs.
  C. use tools, factories, and money.
  D. organize production, distribution, and consumption.

_____ **6.** Which of the following is NOT a basic economic decision every society must make?

A. how goods and services should be produced
B. what and how much should be produced
C. what the market price of goods and services should be
D. who should get what is produced

_____ **7.** An economic system in which a central authority makes the decisions is called a

A. market economy.
B. mixed economy.
C. command economy.
D. traditional economy.

_____ **8.** Which is NOT a name for a system in which individuals make the basic economic decisions?

A. free enterprise
B. capitalism
C. command economy
D. market economy

_____ **9.** Where free competition operates, the market works mainly according to

A. laws of supply and demand.
B. laws made by legislatures.
C. supplies of the producers.
D. demands of the labor unions.

_____ **10.** One advantage of a corporation over other kinds of business ownership is that corporations

A. are less expensive to start.
B. are easier to start.
C. are less limited by government regulations.
D. can raise more money.

_____ **11.** Entrepreneurs are important in a market economy because they

A. provide interest on investments.
B. keep corporations from getting too large.
C. take risks to start new businesses.
D. make decisions about who should get goods and services.

_____ **12.** Large corporations are important in the United States for all of the following reasons EXCEPT they

A. usually produce goods and services more efficiently than small businesses.
B. pay about 70 percent of the total wages earned.
C. account for more than 90 percent of the total sales.
D. make up about 90 percent of the businesses in the country.

_____ **13.** Major accomplishments of labor unions include all EXCEPT

A. They helped win fairer wages for workers.
B. They pushed for laws protecting workers.
C. They worked to prevent corporations from making profits.
D. They got the government to provide unemployment insurance.

_____ **14.** Which of the following is NOT a kind of personal income?

A. insurance premiums
B. wages
C. fringe benefits
D. commissions

_____ **15.** When consumers use credit, they

A. receive interest payments on their accounts.
B. stay out of debt.
C. get a discount.
D. trade future buying power for immediate satisfaction.

_____ **16.** A budget can make it easier to manage your money by helping you

A. cut your fixed expenses.
B. plan your spending.
C. increase your income.
D. earn larger dividends.

_____ **17.** In thinking about a career you do NOT need to

A. assume that you are making a lifetime decision.
B. find out what level of education it requires.
C. look into what an employer in that field would expect of you.
D. consider whether it fits your goals and values.

_____ **18.** Our federal government has intervened in the economy in all the following ways EXCEPT to

A. enforce honest advertising.
B. ban state public assistance.
C. enforce safety standards.
D. let small businesses compete.

_____ **19.** An important way the government influences our economy is by

A. controlling who can borrow money.
B. setting prices that can be charged for goods and services.
C. allowing businesses to operate in any way they want.
D. controlling the amount of money in the system.

_____ **20.** Problems in our market economy have led government to do all EXCEPT

A. set a minimum wage.
B. require employers to bargain with unions.
C. require testing of new drugs.
D. require businesses to form trusts.

_____ **21.** If the gross domestic product is rising, it means that
A. the national debt is growing.
B. prices are rising.
C. more goods and services are being produced.
D. fewer goods and services are being produced.

_____ **22.** Proposals for reducing the national debt include all EXCEPT
A. cutting social security benefits.
B. borrowing money.
C. reducing defense spending.
D. raising taxes.

_____ **23.** Our money has value because
A. it can be counted accurately.
B. government stands behind it.
C. it is expensive to produce.
D. people save it.

_____ **24.** The total amount of money available in a country for spending is the
A. currency.
B. bank reserves.
C. money supply.
D. demand deposits.

_____ **25.** Inflation may cause the Federal Reserve System to
A. ban taxation.
B. supply currency.
C. transfer money.
D. discourage loans.

_____ **26.** Which of the following characteristics is NOT true of our money?
A. Its supply can be controlled.
B. It is easily destroyed.
C. It can be counted and measured accurately.
D. It is easy to carry and use.

_____ **27.** The three parts of the money supply in the United States are
A. currency, demand deposits, and traveler's checks.
B. checks, bills, and coins.
C. currency, bonds, and traveler's checks.
D. bonds, currency, and demand deposits.

_____ **28.** Banks can lend money because
A. they pay interest on savings accounts.
B. they sell traveler's checks.
C. they must keep only a fraction of the money people deposit.
D. the Federal Reserve gives it to them.

_____ **29.** The Federal Reserve System tries to

A. encourage recession because it makes things cheaper.

B. maintain a balance between inflation and recession.

C. encourage inflation because it makes property more valuable.

D. stop the business cycle from operating in the United States.

_____ **30.** The Employment Act of 1946 stated that the government would promote all of the following EXCEPT

A. unions.

B. employment.

C. production.

D. purchasing power.

_____ **31.** When government is included in the circular flow of economic activity, this is called a

A. market economy.

B. free enterprise system.

C. traditional economy.

D. mixed economy.

_____ **32.** All are characteristics of a good tax EXCEPT

A. it is efficient and economical.

B. there is a good reason for the tax.

C. it should only be paid by the wealthy.

D. it is convenient to pay and to collect.

_____ **33.** Which statement is true about a balanced budget?

A. The government spends less than it gets from taxes.

B. The government spends only what it receives in taxes.

C. The government spends more than it gets from taxes.

D. All levels of government require it.

_____ **34.** Our society makes laws for all of the following reasons EXCEPT

A. to protect people's safety.

B. to protect people's property.

C. to enforce morals.

D. to protect individual freedoms.

_____ **35.** Laws bring order to our society in all the following ways EXCEPT by

A. spelling out ways to settle conflicts.

B. setting standards.

C. telling people what they may or may not do.

D. giving the government unlimited power.

_____ **36.** Any behavior that is illegal because the government considers it harmful to society is a

A. crime.
B. civil suit.
C. felony.
D. misdemeanor.

_____ **37.** The reason most Americans do not break the law is

A. they do not want to be arrested.
B. the laws are made by experts.
C. the courts are too crowded.
D. the laws reflect their basic values.

_____ **38.** The common goal of both criminal and civil law is to

A. keep criminals off the streets.
B. provide orderly ways to settle disputes.
C. enforce laws.
D. help people live peacefully together.

_____ **39.** Which of the following statements is NOT true of criminal laws?

A. They help settle disagreements.
B. They define acts the government considers harmful to society.
C. They reflect local values.
D. They are organized into codes.

_____ **40.** All of the following are sources of law EXCEPT

A. state legislatures.
B. city councils.
C. police departments.
D. the decisions of judges.

_____ **41.** If a majority of citizens wants to change a law, the citizens

A. should change their own values instead.
B. must rewrite it.
C. can do nothing about it.
D. can elect representatives who will change it.

_____ **42.** A particular action becomes a crime when

A. too many people start doing it.
B. the person doing it is arrested.
C. it hurts the society as a whole.
D. a law is written against it.

_____ **43.** The main purpose of criminal law is to

A. provide rules for filing lawsuits.
B. be sure the law is the same from state to state.
C. help people settle disputes.
D. protect against acts that are harmful to society.

_____ **44.** The main purpose of civil law is to

A. ensure that people obey city ordinances.

B. decide punishments for particular crimes.

C. define crimes.

D. provide a way for people to settle disputes.

_____ **45.** In general, there is more crime in

A. wealthy rural areas.

B. wealthy suburban areas.

C. poor urban areas.

D. poor rural areas.

_____ **46.** In the United States, crime

A. against people happens more often than crime against property.

B. is not seen as a problem by most people.

C. is not a problem if you live in a wealthy neighborhood.

D. costs people, businesses, and governments billions of dollars each year.

_____ **47.** In explaining the causes of crime in the United States, people agree that

A. violence on television encourages violent behavior.

B. poverty leads to crime.

C. the problem has more than one cause.

D. the courts are too easy on criminals.

_____ **48.** The police can arrest

A. only people for whom they have a warrant.

B. anyone they choose to.

C. anyone they have a good reason to believe has committed a crime.

D. only people indicted by the grand jury.

_____ **49.** A grand jury reviews a serious case to be sure there is

A. probable cause.

B. a plea bargain.

C. an informal charge.

D. bail.

_____ **50.** One difference between an adult criminal trial and a juvenile hearing is that at a hearing

A. no witnesses are allowed.

B. there is no jury.

C. there are no attorneys.

D. a jury gives a lighter sentence.

_____ **51.** When a person accused of a crime comes to trial, all of the following rights are protected EXCEPT the right

A. to question any witnesses called by the prosecution.

B. to call witnesses.

C. to tell a lie to protect himself or herself.

D. not to testify.

_____ **52.** The goal of juvenile courts is to

A. prosecute status offenders.

B. help children in trouble.

C. keep trouble-making children off the streets.

D. punish children who commit crimes.

_____ **53.** A juvenile who is arrested for a crime

A. has a hearing instead of a trial.

B. goes through the same steps as an adult.

C. is put in prison.

D. is automatically placed on probation.

_____ **54.** Our civil justice system is based on the idea that

A. people should be taught to live useful lives.

B. wrongdoers must be punished.

C. people are responsible for any harm they have done.

D. the rights of people accused of crime must be protected.

_____ **55.** Which of the following is NOT true of a civil lawsuit?

A. The defendant must be found guilty beyond a reasonable doubt.

B. It begins when the plaintiff files a complaint.

C. The case may be settled out of court.

D. Evidence is gathered through discovery.

_____ **56.** One of the biggest problems of the civil justice system is that

A. the defendant risks going to prison.

B. jurors are hard to find.

C. the trials are unfair.

D. lawsuits often take too long to settle.

_____ **57.** One way courts settle civil cases is through

A. enforcing probation.

B. fining the person who loses the lawsuit.

C. putting the guilty party in jail.

D. payment of damages to make up for a loss.

_____ **58.** All of the following problems can be settled in civil court EXCEPT
A. disputes between renters and landlords.
B. conflicts over contracts.
C. accusations of larceny.
D. disagreements over property.

_____ **59.** One difference between civil and criminal trials is that in a civil trial
A. the parties have more at risk.
B. the evidence must be heard by a jury.
C. wrongdoing can be proven by a preponderance of the evidence.
D. wrongdoing cannot be proven by a preponderance of the evidence.

_____ **60.** Civil trials often take a long time to settle because
A. people find other ways to settle their conflicts.
B. arbitration slows down the process.
C. there are not enough judges and courtrooms.
D. plaintiffs drop cases they cannot win.

_____ **61.** People can avoid a civil trial but still settle conflicts by using any of the following methods EXCEPT
A. arbitration.
B. mediation.
C. criminal trials.
D. private judges.

_____ **62.** Even if a person has decided to go ahead with a civil trial, he or she can sometimes reduce the cost by
A. hiring a lawyer.
B. becoming an arbitrator.
C. using a small claims court.
D. refusing mediation.

_____ **63.** Which of the following is a role of political parties?
A. minimizing direct involvement to citizens
B. running the mass media
C. organizing the Electoral College
D. nominating candidates for office

_____ **64.** In the United States, political parties seek to influence and control government by
A. eliminating other parties.
B. preventing citizens from playing a direct role in government.
C. getting their candidates elected to office.
D. banding together with other parties.

_____ **65.** One way parties inform people is by

A. canvassing.
B. registering.
C. raising funds.
D. caucusing.

_____ **66.** The first political parties formed over the issue of

A. what economic system to have.
B. whether to expand territory.
C. whether to form a democracy.
D. the role of the government.

_____ **67.** National political party conventions do all the following EXCEPT

A. nominate presidential candidates.
B. approve the party platform.
C. approve the vice-presidential candidate.
D. identify candidates for the Senate.

_____ **68.** Political parties help all Americans in all of the following ways EXCEPT

A. giving them a voice in government.
B. simplifying political decision making.
C. providing special services to members.
D. informing them about issues.

_____ **69.** Our current two-party system

A. formed to support a strong national government.
B. was established by the Constitution.
C. emerged in the mid-1800s.
D. was founded by the Federalists.

_____ **70.** Third parties play an important political role by

A. getting on the ballot in all states.
B. raising money.
C. bringing up new issues and ideas.
D. winning a majority of the votes.

_____ **71.** The two major political parties are similar EXCEPT in their

A. need for broad support.
B. view of the role of government.
C. basic beliefs and values.
D. efforts to attract independent voters.

_____ **72.** Political party organizations operate
- **A.** at the local, state, and national levels.
- **B.** at the national level only.
- **C.** at the local level only.
- **D.** only during presidential campaigns.

_____ **73.** Who runs a political campaign?
- **A.** the Electoral College
- **B.** the poll taker
- **C.** the campaign manager
- **D.** the Federal Election Commission

_____ **74.** In general, major political parties seem to be
- **A.** gaining strength.
- **B.** becoming more numerous.
- **C.** attracting a growing number of young voters.
- **D.** losing strength.

_____ **75.** Which of the following is NOT a way in which candidates for Congress can be nominated?
- **A.** caucus
- **B.** self-nomination
- **C.** direct primary
- **D.** national party convention

_____ **76.** To vote in most states, you must be all of the following EXCEPT
- **A.** present in person.
- **B.** at least 18 years old.
- **C.** a resident of the state in which you vote.
- **D.** registered.

_____ **77.** Voters make final decisions about elected officials and issues at
- **A.** national conventions.
- **B.** voter registration.
- **C.** general elections.
- **D.** primary elections.

_____ **78.** All of the following may be found on a ballot EXCEPT
- **A.** a referendum.
- **B.** names of candidates.
- **C.** party platforms.
- **D.** an initiative.

_____ **79.** Which of the following is the LEAST reliable source of information on a candidate?
- **A.** newspaper articles
- **B.** debates between candidates
- **C.** television advertisements
- **D.** information from nonpartisan organizations

_____ **80.** Interest groups do all of the following EXCEPT
A. endorse candidates.
B. try to get rid of PACs.
C. work to pass or defeat ballot measures.
D. give money to campaigns.

_____ **81.** Propaganda is
A. information gathered by a poll taker.
B. information without bias.
C. meant to influence people's ideas, opinions, or actions.
D. all lies and false information.

_____ **82.** Propaganda techniques include all of the following EXCEPT
A. glittering generalities.
B. name-calling.
C. fund-raising.
D. card stacking.

_____ **83.** A presidential candidate may NOT use
A. public opinion polls.
B. money from both public funds and PACs.
C. the media.
D. a staff led by a campaign manager.

_____ **84.** The Electoral College
A. was established by the Constitution.
B. seeks to educate young voters.
C. makes voting in general elections unnecessary.
D. does not affect the outcome of elections.

_____ **85.** Which of the following is NOT a goal of American foreign policy?
A. to decrease trade
B. to promote prosperity
C. to protect citizens' safety
D. to work for peace

_____ **86.** Foreign aid helps meet American foreign policy goals by
A. reducing the chances of revolution and war.
B. causing poor nations to turn to communist governments.
C. helping strong nations take over weak nations.
D. all of the above.

_____ **87.** Most developing nations
A. are highly industrialized.
B. never had resources of their own.
C. have more jobs than workers.
D. were once colonies.

_____ **88.** All of the following are basic causes of war EXCEPT
A. unrest within a country.
B. a long-standing quarrel between peoples.
C. arms control.
D. fear of attack.

_____ **89.** The term détente referred to
A. an attempt to stop the spread of communism.
B. a war fought with words and warnings.
C. a "hot" war between Soviet and American allies.
D. a lessening of tensions between the superpowers.

_____ **90.** As a result of the end of the Cold War, the United States
A. can return to isolationism.
B. no longer faces a serious threat to its national security.
C. faces new foreign policy decisions.
D. is no longer a superpower.

_____ **91.** The global economy is an example of growing
A. traditionalism.
B. national sovereignty.
C. interdependence.
D. threats to peace.

_____ **92.** American foreign policy goals include all EXCEPT
A. world peace.
B. aggression.
C. human rights.
D. national security.

_____ **93.** Which of the following is NOT a tool of American foreign policy?
A. democracy
B. defense
C. intelligence
D. trade measures

_____ **94.** The major responsibility for making foreign policy belongs to the
A. Department of State.
B. President.
C. Senate.
D. National Security Council.

_____ **95.** Congress has all of the following powers over foreign policy EXCEPT
A. appointing diplomats.
B. budget-making.
C. approving or rejecting treaties.
D. declaring war.

_____ **96.** Changes in former communist countries have caused policymakers to face questions of how to
A. strengthen containment.
B. encourage democratic change.
C. maintain the cold war.
D. discourage glasnost.

_____ **97.** Which of the following is NOT one of the three basic characteristics of a nation?

A. having territory with borders
B. having one common language
C. having sovereignty
D. having a government

_____ **98.** Which of the following does NOT help a nation protect its national interest?

A. a low standard of living
B. military strength
C. a strong economy
D. valuable resources

_____ **99.** One reason colonial powers wanted colonies was to

A. learn from the native peoples.
B. have a traditional economy.
C. bring more citizens back to their country.
D. gain raw materials and natural resources.

_____ **100.** All of the following powers are part of a nation's sovereignty EXCEPT the power to

A. carry out laws within the nation's borders.
B. deal with other governments.
C. set up colonies in neighboring countries.
D. control who may enter its territory.

_____ **101.** A developed nation is more likely than a developing nation to have

A. a high standard of living.
B. an economy based on agriculture.
C. high unemployment.
D. not enough schools.

_____ **102.** Which of the following is a sign of interdependence?

A. Competition is a normal part of the way nations interact.
B. Most colonies have become independent nations.
C. The arms race picked up speed in the early 1980s.
D. Much of what you consume is made in other countries.

_____ **103.** All of the following are true of the United Nations EXCEPT that it

A. has sovereignty over members.
B. uses military forces.
C. cannot make laws that must be obeyed.
D. resembles a national government.

_____**104.** The United Nations has had its greatest successes in

A. dealing with political problems.

B. dealing with economic problems.

C. creating regional organizations.

D. enforcing international law.

_____**105.** The United Nations

A. cannot make laws.

B. has sovereignty over its member nations.

C. has the power to enforce international law.

D. cannot recommend trade measures.

Name ______________________ Date __________________ Class ____________

Whole-Course Exam

Multiple Choice

Identify the letter of the choice that best completes the statement or answers the question.

_____ **1.** Which of the following are values?

A. equality, ideals, beliefs
B. diversity, beliefs, equality
C. freedom, diversity, ideals
D. equality, freedom, justice

_____ **2.** The most basic institution in any society is the

A. family.
B. government.
C. school.
D. church.

_____ **3.** The basic American value of equality means that

A. anyone can hold elective office.
B. racism does not exist.
C. everyone is equally good at things.
D. everyone should have the same rights and opportunities.

_____ **4.** All of the following are American economic freedoms EXCEPT

A. the freedom to choose an occupation.
B. the freedom to buy and sell.
C. the freedom to own property.
D. the freedom to not be a consumer.

_____ **5.** A citizen of the United States must

A. defend the nation.
B. be a church member.
C. join important civic clubs.
D. read the newspaper.

_____ **6.** Your rights as a citizen include

A. the right to refuse to serve on a jury.
B. the right to say what you think in writing.
C. the right to use your personal property any way you want.
D. unlimited freedom.

_____ **7.** You are an American citizen if any of the following is true EXCEPT

A. you were born in another country and were over 18 years old when your parents were naturalized.
B. you have been naturalized.
C. at least one of your parents was a United States citizen when you were born.
D. you were born in the United States.

_____ **8.** Our system of government is called a

A. monarchy.
B. democracy.
C. dictatorship.
D. constitutional monarchy.

_____ **9.** The institution of education is important to society for all of the following reasons EXCEPT

A. it helps people meet others with different values.
B. it helps people reach their dreams and goals.
C. it satisfies people's wants and needs for goods and services.
D. it teaches the beliefs and values that hold us together as a society.

_____ **10.** Learning how to be a member of a group is called

A. social interaction.
B. socialization.
C. society.
D. socializing.

_____ **11.** All of the following are true about discrimination EXCEPT

A. it is unfair.
B. it denies equal opportunities to people.
C. it is a result of racism.
D. it no longer occurs in the United States.

_____ **12.** In the colonies the right to vote was held by

A. anyone who could read and write.
B. white men who owned a certain amount of land.
C. men and women over the age of 21.
D. all men.

_____ **13.** The colonists established public schools because they wanted people to

A. work hard.
B. farm productively.
C. be good soldiers.
D. read and understand the Bible.

_____ **14.** The best example of a direct democracy would be

A. the House of Representatives voting on a bill.
B. the Senate voting on a treaty.
C. the student council meeting to choose school colors.
D. the students in a classroom voting on party refreshments.

_____ **15.** Tyranny can occur in

A. a dictatorship.
B. republic.
C. any form of government.
D. a monarchy.

_____ **16.** The Articles of Confederation needed to be revised for all of the following reasons EXCEPT that the Congress

A. needed more power to deal with other nations.

B. could not raise enough money for the government.

C. agreed on what new form of government was needed.

D. could not enforce the laws.

_____ **17.** Federalism is the principle of

A. division of power between the state and national governments.

B. giving each branch of government ways to limit the power of the other branches.

C. checks and balances.

D. separation of powers within the federal government.

_____ **18.** The main argument for adding the Bill of Rights was that it would

A. make more people vote in favor of the Constitution.

B. give the new government more power to free the country from England.

C. make the Constitution more like the English Constitution.

D. gain support for the new government.

_____ **19.** The main argument against the Bill of Rights was that it

A. was unpopular with the people and would cause the Constitution to be defeated.

B. limited the power of the people too much.

C. was not needed.

D. was unconstitutional.

_____ **20.** Your right to get a group of people together to ask the government to change a law is protected by

A. the Fifth Amendment.

B. the First Amendment.

C. the Fourth Amendment.

D. the Sixth Amendment.

_____ **21.** When we say that the First Amendment makes possible a "marketplace of ideas," we mean that

A. the government may not establish any religion.

B. the government must treat people accused of crimes fairly.

C. all views, even unpopular ones, may be expressed in this country.

D. newspapers may print anything they choose to print.

_____ **22.** The amendment that gave African American men the right to vote was the

A. Twenty-fourth.

B. Fifteenth.

C. Thirteenth.

D. Fourteenth.

_____ **23.** The group that gained the right to vote most recently is

A. men and women between the ages of 18 and 21.

B. African Americans.

C. immigrants.

D. women.

_____ **24.** The decision in *Brown* v. *Board of Education of Topeka* called for

A. equal protection of the law.

B. affirmative action.

C. the separate but equal doctrine.

D. segregation.

_____ **25.** The fact that the Constitution has been amended more than 20 times indicates that it

A. should be rewritten entirely.

B. was not a good plan of government.

C. is flexible.

D. is finally perfect.

Using Primary Sources

Use the excerpts from the Declaration of Independence below to choose the letter of the best answer.

Excerpt 1

We hold these truths to be self-evident, that all men are created equal, that they are endowed by their Creator with certain unalienable rights, that among these are life, liberty, and the pursuit of happiness. That, to secure these rights, governments are instituted among men, deriving their just powers from the consent of the governe**D.** That, whenever any form of government becomes destructive of these ends, it is the right of the people to alter or to abolish it. . . .

Excerpt 2

Prudence, indeed, will dictate that governments long established should not be changed for light and transient causes; and, accordingly, all experience has shown that mankind are more disposed to suffer, while evils are sufferable, than to right themselves by abolishing the forms to which they are accustomed.

Excerpt 3

But when a long train of abuses and "usurpations . . . evinces" a design to reduce them under absolute despotism, it is their right, it is their duty, to throw off such government, and to provide new guards for their future security.

Excerpt 4

We, therefore, the representatives of the United States of America, in General Congress assembled, appealing to the Supreme Judge of the world for the rectitude of our intentions, do, in the name and by authority of the good people of these colonies, solemnly publish and declare, that these united colonies are and of right ought to be free and independent states; that they are absolved from all allegiance to the British Crown, and that all political connection between them and the state of Great Britain is and ought to be totally dissolved.

_____ **26.** Excerpt 1 says that governments are
- **A.** given their power by the agreement of the people.
- **B.** the possessors of certain rights that cannot be taken away.
- **C.** generally destructive.
- **D.** created by God to protect people's rights.

_____ **27.** Excerpt 2 says that people
- **A.** want to get rid of slavery.
- **B.** should change their government whenever they wish.
- **C.** will put up with a lot before they try to change government.
- **D.** usually want new governments.

_____ **28.** Excerpt 3 says that
- **A.** kings should be eliminated.
- **B.** people have a duty to create good governments.
- **C.** people need security forces.
- **D.** any government would be better than the British government.

_____ **29.** Excerpt 4 says that the Declaration of Independence was written by
A. representatives of the people of the colonies.
B. the Congress.
C. the Supreme Court.
D. all the people of the colonies.

_____ **30.** Excerpt 4 says that the people of the United States
A. will create a new monarchy.
B. declare their independence.
C. intend to go to war against Great Britain to gain independence.
D. ally themselves with Great Britain.

_____ **31.** Congress does NOT have the power to
A. spend money.
B. declare war.
C. create federal courts.
D. appoint ambassadors.

_____ **32.** Congressional committees do all of the following EXCEPT
A. recommend bills for a vote in the House or Senate.
B. send bills to the President to sign.
C. conduct investigations.
D. study and hold public hearings on bills.

_____ **33.** In order to become a law, a bill must be
A. passed by both houses of Congress.
B. vetoed by the President.
C. approved by both political parties.
D. approved by the Supreme Court.

_____ **34.** The President's most important job is to
A. set national goals and develop foreign and domestic policies.
B. represent the voters.
C. make laws.
D. direct the bureaucracy.

_____ **35.** The President can carry out policies in all the following ways EXCEPT by
A. giving executive orders.
B. making executive agreements.
C. making laws.
D. appointing Supreme Court justices.

_____ **36.** To appoint people to many positions, the President needs the approval of

A. the House of Representatives.
B. the Supreme Court.
C. the Senate.
D. the executive branch.

_____ **37.** "Executive privilege" means that the President

A. entertains visiting foreign leaders.
B. may make trade agreements without approval by Congress.
C. must be obeyed by members of the bureaucracy.
D. may keep some information secret from Congress and the courts.

_____ **38.** Which of the following events occurs first in the life of a law?

A. A conference committee is formed.
B. Both houses of Congress pass a bill.
C. The President signs a bill into law.
D. A senator or representative proposes a bill.

_____ **39.** The defendant in a trial is

A. on the same side as the prosecution.
B. the person against whom a complaint is brought.
C. also known as the plaintiff.
D. usually not known at the beginning of a trial.

_____ **40.** The Supreme Court uses its power of judicial review when it

A. hears cases involving disputes between state governments.
B. chooses which appeals cases to hear.
C. follows precedent.
D. rules that a law is unconstitutional.

_____ **41.** Checks on the judicial branch include all of the following EXCEPT

A. the Senate's power to confirm judicial appointments.
B. the President's power to remove justices.
C. the power of Congress to propose constitutional amendments.
D. the President's power to appoint judges.

_____ **42.** The system of dividing power between the state and federal governments is called

A. checks and balances.
B. federalism.
C. a more perfect union.
D. separation of powers.

_____ **43.** State governments have the power
- **A.** to set up public schools.
- **B.** to declare war.
- **C.** to coin money.
- **D.** to make treaties with other countries.

_____ **44.** Seats in the upper houses of state legislatures are apportioned on the basis of
- **A.** number of people.
- **B.** tradition.
- **C.** number of voters.
- **D.** geographic area.

_____ **45.** Which of the following does NOT give citizens direct power over state government?
- **A.** the constitutional initiative
- **B.** the item veto
- **C.** the recall
- **D.** the referendum

_____ **46.** Certificates the government sells and agrees to pay interest on are called
- **A.** bonds.
- **B.** deposits.
- **C.** loans.
- **D.** excises.

_____ **47.** The executive branch of state government is headed by
- **A.** the assembly.
- **B.** the Supreme Court.
- **C.** the Cabinet.
- **D.** the governor.

_____ **48.** Governors usually have the most control over the
- **A.** other top executive branch officials.
- **B.** legislature.
- **C.** state constitution.
- **D.** budget.

_____ **49.** Which of the following determines the powers of a local government?
- **A.** the national Constitution
- **B.** Congress
- **C.** the state government
- **D.** a board of supervisors

_____ **50.** Counties are usually governed by
- **A.** a county clerk.
- **B.** a mayor and council.
- **C.** an elected board.
- **D.** a sheriff.

_____ **51.** The local government plan that does NOT include a mayor is called the
- **A.** home rule plan.
- **B.** council plan.
- **C.** weak-mayor plan.
- **D.** commission plan.

_____ **52.** The plan for local government that most closely resembles the federal government is called the

A. commission plan.
B. council-manager plan.
C. home rule plan.
D. mayor-council plan.

_____ **53.** Local governments spend most of their revenue on

A. jails.
B. parks.
C. education.
D. utilities.

_____ **54.** Local and state governments cooperate in all the following EXCEPT

A. paying for education.
B. providing health care.
C. building roads.
D. electing mayors.

_____ **55.** All of the following are true about the factors of production EXCEPT

A. people use them to produce goods and services.
B. people use them to satisfy wants.
C. they include land, labor, and capital.
D. they are unlimited.

_____ **56.** Over time, people's economic wants and needs are

A. mainly for food, clothing, and shelter.
B. the same in every country.
C. easily satisfied.
D. greater than the resources available to satisfy them.

Analyzing Statistical Tables

Use the table below to choose the best answer.

Governments in the United States

Type of government	Number of governments	Number of elected officials	Average number of officials per government
Federal	1	542	542
State	50	18,828	377
Local	84,995	493,830	6
County	3,043	58,818	19
Municipal	19,279	135,531	7
Township	16,656	126,958	8
School district	14,422	88,434	6
Other special district	31,555	84,089	3
Total	**85,006**	**513,200**	**6**

Source: U.S. Bureau of the Census

_____ **57.** Of the following, which is the most common form of local government?

A. municipal
B. township
C. county
D. school district

_____ **58.** Of the types of local government, which has the greatest total number of elected officials?

A. municipal
B. county
C. school district
D. township

_____ **59.** Which of the following types of local government has the greatest average number of officials?

A. school district
B. municipal
C. township
D. county

_____ **60.** An economic system is a way for a society to

A. make profits from investments.
B. train workers for future jobs.
C. use tools, factories, and money.
D. organize production, distribution, and consumption.

_____ **61.** An economic system in which a central authority makes the decisions is called a

A. market economy.
B. mixed economy.
C. command economy.
D. traditional economy.

_____ **62.** According to the law of demand,
- **A.** money flows in a circle.
- **B.** people will usually demand higher wages.
- **C.** the government decides who gets what is produced.
- **D.** when a product's price drops, people will often buy more of it.

_____ **63.** Entrepreneurs are important in a market economy because they
- **A.** provide interest on investments.
- **B.** keep corporations from getting too large.
- **C.** take risks to start new businesses.
- **D.** make decisions about who should get goods and services.

_____ **64.** Major accomplishments of labor unions include all EXCEPT
- **A.** They helped win fairer wages for workers.
- **B.** They pushed for laws protecting workers.
- **C.** They worked to prevent corporations from making profits.
- **D.** They got the government to provide unemployment insurance.

_____ **65.** Which of the following is NOT a kind of personal income?
- **A.** insurance premiums
- **C.** fringe benefits
- **B.** wages
- **D.** commissions

ANALYZING LINE GRAPHS

Use the graph below to choose the best answer.

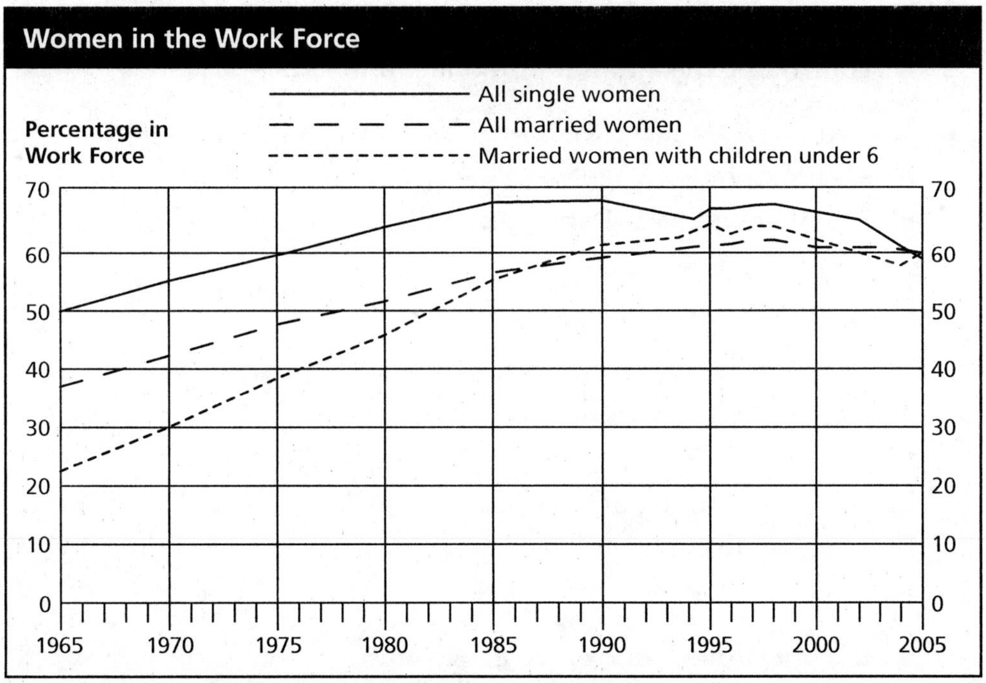

Source: *A Field Guide to the U.S. Economy,* Bureau of Labor Statistics

_____ **66.** In 1965 the percentage of married women who had children under age 6 and who worked outside the home was

A. less than 10 percent.
B. approximately 25 percent.
C. almost 40 percent.
D. about 50 percent.

_____ **67.** More than 50 percent of the women in all the groups shown had entered the work force by

A. 1985.
B. 1970.
C. 1980.
D. 1975.

_____ **68.** During the time period covered by the graph, which group had the largest percentage increase entering the work force?

A. married women with children under age 6
B. married women without children
C. married women
D. single women

_____ **69.** Of the following questions, which is the only one the graph can answer?

A. What percentage of women held service jobs in 1995?
B. Why did more women with young children take jobs?
C. How many women worked in 1970?
D. What percentage of single women worked in 1990?

_____ **70.** An important way the government influences our economy is by
A. controlling who can borrow money.
B. setting prices that can be charged for goods and services.
C. allowing businesses to operate in any way they want.
D. controlling the amount of money in the system.

_____ **71.** Problems in our market economy have led government to do all EXCEPT
A. set a minimum wage.
B. require employers to bargain with unions.
C. require testing of new drugs.
D. require businesses to form trusts.

_____ **72.** Which of the following characteristics is NOT true of our money?
A. Its supply can be controlled.
B. It is easily destroyed.
C. It can be counted and measured accurately.
D. It is easy to carry and use.

_____ **73.** Banks can lend money because
A. they pay interest on savings accounts.
B. they sell traveler's checks.
C. they must keep only a fraction of the money people deposit.
D. the Federal Reserve gives it to them.

_____ **74.** The Federal Reserve System tries to
A. encourage recession because it makes things cheaper.
B. maintain a balance between inflation and recession.
C. encourage inflation because it makes property more valuable.
D. stop the business cycle from operating in the United States.

_____ **75.** The process by which our nation keeps track of our overall income and spending is
A. national income accounting.
B. the office of accounting.
C. certified public accounting.
D. the office of budget management.

_____ **76.** The methods of determining income taxes include all of the following EXCEPT
A. progressive tax.
B. regressive tax.
C. proportional tax.
D. sales tax.

_____ **77.** Examples of entitlement programs include all of the following EXCEPT
A. Social Security.
B. Medicare.
C. the Bill of Rights.
D. Medicaid.

_____ **78.** Our society makes laws for all of the following reasons EXCEPT
A. to protect people's safety.
B. to protect people's property.
C. to enforce morals.
D. to protect people's individual freedoms.

_____ **79.** The common goal of both criminal and civil law is to
A. keep criminals off the streets.
B. provide orderly ways to settle disputes.
C. enforce laws.
D. help people live peacefully together.

_____ **80.** If a majority of citizens wants to change a law, the citizens
A. should change their own values instead.
B. must rewrite it.
C. can do nothing about it.
D. can elect representatives who will change it.

_____ **81.** A particular action becomes a crime when
A. too many people start doing it.
B. a law is written against it.
C. it hurts the society as a whole.
D. the person doing it is arrested.

_____ **82.** The main purpose of criminal law is to
A. provide rules for filing lawsuits.
B. be sure the law is the same from state to state.
C. help people settle disputes.
D. protect against acts that are harmful to society.

_____ **83.** The main purpose of civil law is to
A. ensure that people obey city ordinances.
B. decide punishments for particular crimes.
C. define crimes.
D. provide a way for people to settle disputes.

_____ **84.** The police can arrest

A. only people for whom they have a warrant.

B. anyone they choose to.

C. anyone they have a good reason to believe has committed a crime.

D. only people indicted by the grand jury.

_____ **85.** When a person accused of a crime comes to trial, all of the following rights are protected EXCEPT the right

A. to question any witnesses called by the prosecution.

B. to call witnesses.

C. to tell a lie to protect himself or herself.

D. not to testify.

_____ **86.** The goal of juvenile courts is to

A. prosecute status offenders.

B. help children in trouble.

C. keep trouble-making children off the streets.

D. punish children who commit crimes.

_____ **87.** One way courts settle civil cases is through

A. enforcing probation.

B. fining the person who loses the lawsuit.

C. putting the guilty party in jail.

D. payment of damages to make up for a loss.

_____ **88.** All of the following problems can be settled in civil court EXCEPT

A. disputes between renters and landlords.

B. conflicts over contracts.

C. accusations of larceny.

D. disagreements over property.

_____ **89.** One difference between civil and criminal trials is that in a civil trial

A. the parties have more at risk.

B. the evidence must be heard by a jury.

C. wrongdoing can be proven by a preponderance of the evidence.

D. wrongdoing cannot be proven by a preponderance of the evidence.

_____ **90.** People can avoid a civil trial but still settle conflicts by using any of the following methods EXCEPT

A. criminal trials.

B. mediation.

C. arbitration.

D. private judges.

Analyzing Statistical Tables

Use the table below to choose the best answer.

Typical Lengths of Parts of Some Criminal Jury Trials* (in hours and minutes)				
	Narcotics	**Assault**	**Robbery**	**Homicide**
Jury Selection	2:00	2:11	3:00	8:14
Prosecutor's Case	2:49	4:06	3:41	13:43
Defense Case	1:30	1:47	1:40	4:38
Jury Deliberation	2:12	2:38	1:50	5:30

*Based on data gathered from over 1,500 trials in New Jersey and California
Source: *On Trial: The Length of Civil and Criminal Trials.* Williamsburg National Center for State Courts

_____ **91.** In which type of trial does the selection of the jury usually take the least time?

A. robbery
B. homicide
C. narcotics
D. assault

_____ **92.** The type of trial that takes the longest time overall usually involves

A. narcotics.
B. homicide.
C. assault.
D. robbery.

_____ **93.** The side that takes the longest to present its case is the side that wants to show

A. the innocence of the defendant.
B. the guilt of the defendant.
C. the guilt of the plaintiff.
D. the innocence of the plaintiff.

_____ **94.** From the data, you can conclude ONLY that, typically,

A. homicide trials generally take longer than other trials.
B. there are twice as many narcotics trials as assault trials.
C. narcotics cases are not as important as robbery cases.
D. defense attorneys do not try very hard in narcotics cases.

_____ **95.** Which of the following is a role of political parties?

A. minimizing direct involvement to citizens
B. running the mass media
C. organizing the Electoral College
D. nominating candidates for office

_____ **96.** Political parties help all Americans in all of the following ways EXCEPT
A. giving them a voice in government.
B. simplifying political decision making.
C. providing special services to members.
D. informing them about issues.

_____ **97.** Third parties play an important political role by
A. getting on the ballot in all states.
B. raising money.
C. bringing up new issues and ideas.
D. winning a majority of the votes.

_____ **98.** The two major political parties are similar EXCEPT in their
A. need for broad support.
B. view of the role of government.
C. basic beliefs and values.
D. efforts to attract independent voters.

_____ **99.** In general, major political parties seem to be
A. gaining strength.
B. becoming more numerous.
C. attracting a growing number of young voters.
D. losing strength.

_____ **100.** Which of the following is NOT a way in which candidates for Congress can be nominated?
A. caucus
B. self-nomination
C. direct primary
D. national party convention

_____ **101.** Voters make final decisions about elected officials and issues at
A. national conventions.
B. voter registration.
C. general elections.
D. primary elections.

_____ **102.** Which of the following is the LEAST reliable source of information on a candidate?
A. newspaper articles
B. debates between candidates
C. television advertisements
D. information from nonpartisan organizations

_____**103.** Interest groups do all of the following EXCEPT

A. endorse candidates.

B. try to get rid of PACs.

C. work to pass or defeat ballot measures.

D. give money to campaigns.

_____**104.** All of the following are goals of American foreign policy EXCEPT

A. building a strong military.

B. stopping terrorism.

C. increasing trade.

D. preventing wars.

_____**105.** One American agency that gathers intelligence about other countries is the

A. United Nations

B. the OAS

C. the OECD.

D. the CIA

_____**106.** Which of the following plays the major role in making and carrying out foreign policy?

A. the executive branch

B. Congress

C. the Supreme Court.

D. businesses

_____**107.** The UN has had some of its greatest successes in dealing with

A. political problems.

B. economic problems.

C. international conflicts.

D. establishing international laws.

Unit 1 Foundations of Citizenship

Key Terms

alien A citizen of one country who lives in another country
baby boom Dramatic rise in the number of births that occurred between 1946 and 1964
beliefs Certain ideas that we trust are true
blended families Families made up of adults and their children from previous marriages
candidate person running for office
census A population survey that is taken every ten years
citizen A person with certain rights and duties under a government.
common good The well being of all members of society
consumer A person who uses, or consumes, goods and services to satisfy his or her wants
democracy A system in which the power is shared by all the people
demography The study of the size, growth, and distribution of human populations
dictatorship a government controlled by one person
discrimination The unfair treatment of a group of people compared with another group
diversity Differences
economy A system for producing and distributing goods and services to fulfill people's wants
equality The condition of everyone having the same rights and opportunities
exclusion laws Prohibited any further immigration from China and Japan
family The most basic social institution in any society
freedom The ability to make choices
goods Physical products
immigrants People who move from one country to make their homes in another
jury of peers Group of ordinary citizens who hear a case and decide whether an accused person is innocent or guilty
justice Fairness
market Places where people exchange goods or services
monarchy Form of government in which all or most of the power is in the hands of one individual whose authority is hereditary
money Anything which is generally accepted as payment for a good or a service
naturalization The process of becoming a citizen
patriotism The demonstration of love and devotion to one's country
political socialization The process of learning how to behave politically
price The amount you must pay for a good or service in a market
racism The belief that members of one's own race are superior to those of other races
representatives People who are chosen to speak and act for their fellow citizens in government
rule of law Concept of a government of laws, rather than of men and women
rules Specific expectations about what our behavior should be
service job Jobs in which a person makes a living by providing a service for other people
services Work you pay to have done
social institutions Systems of values and rules that determine how our society is organized
socialization The process of learning how to participate in a group
social roles Roles that people play in real life
Sunbelt Warm weather states such as Georgia, Florida, Texas, and Arizona
values Our standards of behavior
witnesses People who have seen events related to a crime or who have special information that may help determine the guilt or innocence of the person on trial

Basic American Values

Value	Description
Equality	A social arrangement or condition or circumstance in which everyone has the same rights and opportunities
Freedom	The ability to say what you want, go where you want, and do what you want
Justice	Fairness; the idea that everyone deserves to be treated fairly

Common Forms of Government

Form	Description
Democracy	A political system in which power is shared by all the people. By voting and choosing representatives, the people decide how their government will meet needs and protect rights and freedoms.
Dictatorship	A government controlled by one person—a dictator, who usually takes power by force rather than by inheriting it.
Monarchy	A form of government in which all or most of the power is in the hands of one individual, the monarch, whose authority is inherited.

Ways Society Is Organized

Every society has five major institutions to satisfy needs and teach values and to provide a framework within which groups and organizations exist. Society is organized in different ways to meet the needs of its citizens.

Social Institution	Function	What Needs Are Met
Family	The most basic institution in any society	Makes individuals feel secure (safe and protected); provides a sense of belonging
Religion	Organization with a moral code and spiritual orientation; a community of people who have similar goals and similar ways of looking at life	Gives individuals a sense of community; a source of guidance and support
Education	Institution that equips children with skills and rules required to live in the world	Serves society's needs by training citizens to do work; provides individuals with a comfortable life and a sense of being a worthwhile person
The economy	The system for producing and distributing goods and services to fulfill people's wants	Responds to people's wants; includes a set of rules and expectations
Government	Institution that maintains law and order	Provides law, order, and national security

Economic Freedoms

Freedom	Description
Buy and sell	The freedom to sell a product to anyone you wish at whatever price; every person has the freedom to buy or not to buy a product
Compete	Freedom to make and sell a product; the freedom to compete; the freedom to make and sell more or better products
Make a profit	If people are willing to pay more for a product than it costs to make it, a profit will result; profits encourage people to produce goods and services
Own property	Products are property that are owned until sold; the right to own property and to buy and sell and use it as you wish is a basic rule of the American economic system
Choose an occupation	Freedom to pursue any career

The Need for Government

Need	Function
Law and Order	Government makes and enforces laws that protect rights and ensure that people's lives can proceed in a peaceful, orderly way. Through courts, our government can also settle disputes and punish lawbreakers.
Security	Government provides for our common defense against outside attack by maintaining armed forces and weapons. Our government makes treaties with other countries in which both sides agree to keep the peace or to help each other in case of attack.
Public Services	Government provides services we need but cannot depend on private business to provide. Such services include building and maintaining roads, sewers, and schools.
Maintaining Other Institutions	Government can help to maintain the other institutions in society. For example, in the United States, government protects our freedom of religion, pays for our schools, and provides hundreds of services for families from health care to issuing marriage licenses.

Rights, Duties, and Responsibilities of Citizens

Rights	• To vote and hold elected office • To say what you think in speech or in writing • To practice your own religion • To have a fair trial • To be protected by your government when you are working or traveling in other countries
Duties	**Obeying the laws** Society's formal, or written, rules are laws. Some laws keep people from hurting one another; others protect the rights of citizens. Still other laws establish the rules for making agreements and for settling disagreements in a fair and peaceful way. **Defending the nation** Helping our country defend itself against threats to peace and security is another important duty of citizens. **Serving on a jury or as a witness in court** Our Constitution guarantees that anyone accused of a crime may have the case decided by a jury of peers, a group of ordinary citizens who hear the case and decide whether the accused person is innocent or guilty. **Paying taxes** Through taxes, our local, state, and national governments raise money to pay for the services that citizens ask them to provide. **Attending school** One purpose of school attendance laws is to make sure that young people are prepared to support themselves and to contribute to our economy. Another important task of the schools is to give students the knowledge, skills, and experiences they need to carry out the duties and responsibilities of the "office of citizen."
Responsibilities	**The common good** The basic responsibility of every citizen is to contribute to the common good, or the well-being of all members of society. **Voting** Voting is one of the most important responsibilities of citizenship. Citizens have the responsibility to inform themselves about candidates and issues so that they can make decisions based on reason rather than personal bias. **Holding government office** The people who agree to hold government office are fulfilling another important responsibility of citizenship. They learn about the issues and try to make decisions that are in the best interests of people they represent. **Election campaigns** One of the important ways to fulfill the responsibilities of a citizen is to work on an election campaign. **Influencing government** Citizens are responsible for working to get the government to take action in causes in which they believe. **Serving the community** Americans are responsible for doing whatever they can to make communities better places in which to live.

Unit 2 Creating a Lasting Government

Key Terms

affirmative action Steps to counteract the effects of past racial discrimination and discrimination against women

amendment process The way in which changes are added to the Constitution

amendments Changes

Anti-Federalists Early opponents of the Constitution

bicameral Two-house governmental structure or organization

Bill of Rights A list of citizens' rights

case studies Descriptions of situations or conflicts, the issues involved, and the decisions made toward solution

charter A document giving permission to create a government

checks and balances System that gives each branch of government ways to limit the powers of the other two

compact A written agreement to make and obey laws for the welfare of the group

concurrent powers Powers shared by the federal and state governments

convention assembly

direct democracy A form of government in which laws are made directly by the citizens

double jeopardy Being placed on trial twice for the same crime

due process of law A process by which the government must treat accused persons fairly according to rules established by law

eminent domain The power to take private property for public use

equal protection Idea that people must be treated fairly; does not mean that everyone must be treated in exactly the same way

federalism The division of power between the states and the federal, or national, government

Federalists Early supporters of the Constitution

freedom of the press The right to publish newspapers, magazines, and other materials without governmental restriction

freedom of speech The right to express one's opinions publicly

Great Compromise Plan that gave the large states more power in the House of Representatives, but each state had equal power in the Senate

heritage The traditions passed down to us from generation to generation.

impeach Accuse

legislature A group of people chosen to make the laws

natural rights Rights people are born with and that no government can take away

poll tax Fee for voting

ratification Approval

republic Government in which representatives were elected to make laws

reserved powers Powers that the Constitution neither gives to Congress nor denies to the states

segregation Separation

separation of church and state Situation in which the government may not favor any religion or establish an official religion

separation of powers Dividing government power among legislative, executive, and judicial branches

suffrage The right to vote

Three-Fifths Compromise Plan that counted each slave as three fifths of a person when a state's population was calculated

tyranny Abuse of power

Key Pre-Constitution Documents and Philosophies

Documents and Principles	Description
The Articles of Confederation	Plan drawn up by the Continental Congress for the government of the United States, ratified in 1781.
The common good	Colonial citizens, like citizens today, had a responsibility to work for the common good. They helped their communities in various ways, such as serving on juries, becoming members of the local militia, and supporting education.
The Declaration of Independence	1776 document of "unalienable" rights (rights that no government has the power to take away) and beliefs that the colonists had about these rights; people give power to their government as long as it protects their rights.
The English Bill of Rights	1689 law that further limited the power of the English monarch; included all English citizens, providing that everyone, even government leaders, must obey the law.
Freedom of the press	Although there was no freedom of the press under English law, colonists believed it was necessary to publicly criticize those who abused their power.
Greater religious freedom	Religious freedom for the colonists meant that a person could belong to any Christian church. Considering the world in which they lived, the colonists were taking an important step with these decisions—one that would eventually lead to freedom of religion for all Americans.
Magna Carta	1215 document that was an important step in gaining basic freedoms for all English people, limiting the power of the monarchy by listing rights that the English king or queen had no power to take away; among these rights were the right to a fair trial and the right to travel freely.
Separation of powers	Because power could lead to tyranny, dividing the government among legislative, executive, and judicial branches reduces that possibility, according to French writer Montesquieu, who inspired many colonial leaders.

Basic Principles of the Constitution

Principles of Constitution	Description
Popular sovereignty	The government receives its power from the people and can govern only with their consent.
Limited government	Because the people are the ultimate source of all government power, the government has only as much power as the people give to it.
Separation of powers	The Constitution assigns certain powers to each of the three branches of the government: legislative (Congress), executive (President), and judicial (federal courts).
Checks and balances	The system of checks and balances gives each of the three branches of government the ability to restrain the other two.
Judicial review	The principle of judicial review provides the federal courts with the power to review acts of the federal government and to cancel any acts that are unconstitutional or that violate a provision in the Constitution.
Federalism	A federal system of government is one in which power is divided between a central government and smaller governments.

Articles of the Constitution

Article	Description
Article I: The Legislative Branch	Describes the organization and powers of the national legislature, called the Congress
Article II: The Executive Branch	Gives the power of the executive branch to one person—the President, a leader who has some of the strengths of a monarch but whose authority is based on the consent of the people
Article III: The Judicial Branch	Establishes a national court system that would settle disputes between states; the Supreme Court has final say in all cases involving the Constitution.
Article IV: Relations Among the States	Ensures that the rights of the states are respected; each state must honor the laws of other states.
Article V: Provisions for Amending the Constitution	Creates instructions for making amendments; the framers knew that future Americans might want to change the Constitution.
Article VI: The Supremacy of the Constitution, National Debts, Supremacy of National Law, Oath	Requires officials in state and national government to take an oath to support the Constitution as "the supreme law of the land"; no state law may violate the Constitution.
Article VII: Ratification of the Constitution	Establishes the procedure for ratification, or approval, of the Constitution

Key Supreme Court Cases

Dred Scott v. *Sandford, 1857*

(Sixth Amendment, individual rights) This decision held that Dred Scott, a slave, could not become a free man just because he had traveled in "free soil" states with his master. "Free soil" federal laws and the Missouri Compromise line of 1820 were held unconstitutional because they deprived a slave owner of the right to his "property" without just compensation.

Plessy v. *Ferguson, 1896*

(Fourteenth Amendment, Equal Protection Clause) *Plessy* challenged Louisiana law requiring separate seating for white and African American citizens on public railroads, a form of segregation. The Court held that segregation was permitted if facilities were equal. *Plessy* was overturned by the *Brown* v. *Board of Education* case of 1954.

Brown v. *Board of Education of Topeka, 1954*

(Fourteenth Amendment, Equal Protection Clause) The Court found that segregation in public facilities was a violation of the Equal Protection Clause, commenting that "in the field of public education the doctrine of 'separate but equal' has no place. . . Segregation is a denial of the equal protection of the laws." The decision overturned *Plessy*, 1896.

Tinker v. *Des Moines Public Schools, 1969*

(First Amendment, Free Speech) The Court agreed with the Tinkers, upholding students' First Amendment rights, noting that students do not abandon their civil rights "at the schoolhouse gate . . ." Schools would need to show evidence of the possibility of "substantial disruption" before free speech could be limited at school.

Phillips v. *Martin Marietta Corporation, 1971*

(Fourteenth Amendment, Equal Protection Clause) Phillips was denied a job at Martin Marietta because she had two preschoolers. She charged Martin Marietta with discriminating against women because male applicants were not questioned about their children and were hired whether they had young children or not. The Court ruled that Martin Marietta could not have "one hiring policy for women and another for men."

National Socialist Party of America v. *Skokie, 1977*

(First Amendment, Free Speech) The Court overturned Illinois courts' decisions that forbade anyone to march in a Nazi uniform, display the swastika, or distribute material promoting hatred. The Court concluded that the Nazis had a First Amendment right to wear their symbol, just as war protesters could wear black armbands, as decided in the Tinker case.

Regents of the University of California v. *Bakke, 1978*

(Fourteenth Amendment, Equal Protection Clause) The Court ruled narrowly, providing an admission for Bakke, but not overturning "affirmative action," preferring to take discrimination questions on a case-by-case basis.

Grutter v. *Bollinger, 2003*

(Fourteenth Amendment, Equal Protection Clause) The Court ruled in favor of the University of Michigan. The decision held that no illegal discrimination had occurred when the school accepted minority students with lower test scores than Barbara Grutter, who was denied admission. The majority of judges stated that affirmative action was still needed and therefore schools could consider applicants' race and ethnicity, among other factors.

Amendments to the Constitution

Amendment	Year	Significance
First Amendment	1791	Freedom of religion, speech, press, assembly, and petition
Second Amendment	1791	The right to bear arms
Third Amendment	1791	Quartering of troops not allowed in homes of citizens without owners' consent
Fourth Amendment	1791	No unreasonable searches and seizures
Fifth Amendment	1791	Due process in court; rules for criminal proceedings; eminent domain
Sixth Amendment	1791	Impartial jury, speedy trial, right to a lawyer
Seventh Amendment	1791	Right to a jury trial in lawsuits where more than twenty dollars is at stake
Eighth Amendment	1791	No cruel or unusual punishment, excessive bail, or excessive fines imposed
Ninth Amendment	1791	People have rights not listed in the Constitution.
Tenth Amendment	1791	Limits the power of the federal government; powers not given to the federal government belong to the states and are not listed in the Constitution.
Eleventh Amendment	1798	A private citizen from one state cannot sue the government of another state in federal court; however, a citizen can sue a state government in state court.
Twelfth Amendment	1804	Changed the way the electoral college voted
Thirteenth Amendment	1865	Freed all slaves and forbade involuntary servitude
Fourteenth Amendment	1868	Extended citizenship to blacks; equal protection clause
Fifteenth Amendment	1870	Gave blacks, both former slaves and free blacks, the right to vote
Sixteenth Amendment	1913	Gave Congress the power to collect income taxes without regard to state population
Seventeenth Amendment	1913	Provided that senators are elected directly by the people of each state
Eighteenth Amendment	1919	Banned the making, selling, or transportation of alcoholic beverages in the U.S.
Nineteenth Amendment	1920	Granted women the right to vote
Twentieth Amendment	1933	Set rules for meetings of Congress, commencement of presidential terms, and death or disqualification of presidential candidate
Twenty-first Amendment	1933	Repeal of Prohibition, the Eighteenth Amendment
Twenty-second Amendment	1951	Provided that no President serve more than two terms
Twenty-third Amendment	1961	Gave residents of the District of Columbia the right to vote in presidential elections
Twenty-fourth Amendment	1964	Banned poll taxes in federal elections
Twenty-fifth Amendment	1967	Defined rules for presidential succession and vice presidential appointment
Twenty-sixth Amendment	1971	Established voting age at 18 years
Twenty-seventh Amendment	1992	Congressional pay raises cannot take effect before the next congressional election.

Unit 3 The Federal Government

Key Terms

administration A team of executive branch officials
ambassadors Official representatives to foreign governments
appeal To ask a higher court to review a decision and determine if justice was done
appellate jurisdiction The authority to hear an appeal
bill Proposed law
bill of attainder Law that convicts a person of a crime without a trial
budget Plan for raising and spending money
bureaucracy An organization of government departments, agencies, and offices
Cabinet An important group of policy advisors to the President
census An official count of the population made every ten years
circuit courts Courts of appeal
cloture Agreement to end debate on a bill
congressional district Geographic area a member of the House represents
constituents The people a member of Congress represents
courts of appeal Court that handles appeals from the federal district courts
defendant The party who answers a complaint and defends against it
domestic policy Set of plans for dealing with national problems
executive agreements Agreements with other countries that do not need Senate approval
executive branch Branch of government responsible for executing, or carrying out, the law
executive privilege The right to keep some information secret from Congress and the courts
filibuster Use of long speeches to prevent a vote on a bill
floor leaders Chief officers of the majority and minority parties in each house
foreign policy Set of plans for guiding our nation's relationships with other countries
impeach To accuse an official, such as the President or a federal judge, of serious wrongdoing
interest groups Groups of people who work together for similar interests or goals
judicial activism An effort by judges to take an active role in policymaking by overturning laws relatively often
judicial restraint An effort by judges to avoid overturning laws and to leave policymaking to the other two branches of government
judicial review The power to overturn any law that the Court decides is in conflict with the Constitution
lobbyists People who represent interest groups
opinion A written statement explaining the reasons for a judicial decision
original jurisdiction The authority to hear a case first
plaintiff An individual or a group of people who bring a complaint against another party
pocket veto Situation in which the President pockets, or keeps, a bill for ten days during which Congress ends its session, and the bill does not become law
precedent A legal guideline for deciding similar cases in the future
president pro tempore Person who presides over the Senate when the Vice President is absent
prosecution A government body that brings a criminal charge against a defendant accused of breaking one of its laws
Speaker of the House Presiding officer in the House of Representatives
treaties Formal agreements between nations

Organizations of the Branches of Government

The Executive Branch

The executive branch of government is responsible for executing, or carrying out, the laws.

Members	Description
The President	The President is the leader of the executive branch. The most important duty of the President is to set goals for the nation and to develop policies, which are methods for reaching those goals.
White House staff	The White House staff includes the President's inner circle of trusted advisors and assistants. The staff includes a chief of staff and other key advisors, press secretaries, legal experts, speechwriters, office workers, and researchers.
The Vice President	The Constitution gives the Vice President no duties aside from presiding over the Senate. The President decides what the Vice President will do.
Special advisory groups	Groups that help the President make decisions on domestic and foreign policy; the two most important advisory groups are the Office of Management and Budget (OMB) and the National Security Council (NSC). The OMB decides how much the President's policy goals will cost, while the NSC plays a major role in helping the President make foreign policy.
Executive departments	These form the largest part of the executive branch and do the minute work connected with carrying out the nation's laws and government programs. Executive departments include the Department of State, Department of Treasury, Department of Defense, Department of Agriculture, Department of Justice, and Department of Education.

The Legislative Branch

Congress is the legislative, or lawmaking, branch of the national government. It is made up of two houses: the Senate and the House of Representatives.

Members	Description
Speaker of the House	The Speaker is the most powerful member of the House. The Speaker presides over sessions, deciding the order of business and who may speak, appoints members of committees, and refers bills to committees.
President of the Senate	As presiding officer of the Senate, the Vice President is in charge of Senate sessions but cannot take part in debates and can vote only in case of a tie.
Floor leaders	The chief officers of the majority and minority parties in each house are the floor leaders. Assistant floor leaders, called whips, aid floor leaders in each house.
Standing committees	In both houses of Congress, a bill is sent to a standing committee, which controls the fate of a bill. Each committee deals with a certain area, such as education or banking, and every committee has both Democratic and Republican members. The majority of the members and the chairperson come from the majority party.
Select committees	Sometimes the House or Senate will form a select committee to deal with a problem not covered by any standing committee.
Joint committees	A joint committee is made up of members of both the House and the Senate. Joint committees are usually select committees, formed to conduct investigations.
Conference committees	For each bill, a conference committee is formed to settle differences between House and Senate versions before it goes to the President to be signed.

The Judicial Branch

The judicial branch of the federal government is made up of the Supreme Court and over 100 other federal courts.

Courts	Description
The district courts	As courts of original jurisdiction, the district courts are the first to hear cases such as those involving kidnapping or a city's failure to obey federal air pollution standards.
The courts of appeal	Each court of appeals takes cases from a group of district courts within a particular geographic area called a circuit. The judges decide either to affirm the lower court's decision or to reverse it. There is no jury.
The Supreme Court	The Supreme Court is the highest court in the federal court system. The major purpose of the Supreme Court is to serve as the final court of appeals for both state and federal court systems.
Special federal courts	These special courts include the Court of Claims, the Court of Customs and Patent Appeals, and the Tax Court. Each of these courts was established by Congress for a special purpose.
Federal court judges	All federal judges in the district courts, courts of appeal, and Supreme Court are appointed by the President and confirmed by the Senate. They serve life terms and can be removed from office only by the impeachment process.

Powers of the Branches of Government

The Executive Branch	
The President	• Serves as chief executive, making sure that laws are carried out • Is the leader of the nation's armed forces and makes the most important decisions when the country is at war • Is also our chief diplomat, the most important representative of the United States in relations with other nations • Acts as a legislative leader through policy decisions and through the influence of the veto, as well as the power to call special sessions of Congress • Has the power to choose Supreme Court justices and other federal judges and can limit the power of the judicial branch through pardon
The Legislative Branch	
Legislative powers include the power to	• Collect taxes • Borrow money • Regulate trade with foreign nations and among states • Make laws about naturalization • Coin money and set a standard of weights and measures • Establish post offices and highways • Issue patents and copyrights • Declare war • Create, maintain, and make rules for armed forces • Make laws for the District of Columbia • Make all laws that are "necessary and proper" for carrying out the listed powers
The Judicial Branch	
Judges	• Resolve conflicts by applying laws in situations brought before a court of law • Have the power to interpret the law and may establish a precedent, a guideline for how all similar cases should be decided in the future. A precedent makes the meaning of a law or the Constitution clearer. • Determine how the law should be applied, both inside and outside the legal system

Unit 4 State and Local Government

apportioned Divided among districts
board A group of people who manage the business of an organization
bonds Certificates that people buy from the government
charters Plans of government
councils of governments Groups that work together to meet regional needs
excise tax A charge on certain goods, such as alcoholic beverages, gasoline, and tobacco
federalism The system that divides some powers between the national and state governments while allowing them to share other powers
grant Federal and state governments often give money to local communities
home rule The right of States to write their own charter
impeach Bring charges against
income tax A tax on what individuals and businesses earn
initiative The process by which citizens can propose laws
intergovernmental revenue Money given by one level of government to another
item veto The power to reject particular parts, or items, of a bill
judicial action commissions Official governmental bodies that handle situations in which judges might not be doing their job well
lieutenant governor The state official second in rank to the governor
Missouri Plan A method of choosing judges in which the governor appoints a judge and voters decide whether they want the judge to stay in office
municipality A government that serves people who live in an urban area
ordinances Local laws
property tax A tax on land and buildings
public policy Government response to public issues
recall A process for removing elected officials from office
referendum The process by which a law is referred to the voters to approve or reject
revenue Income
sales tax Charges made on purchases of goods and services
unitary system System in which practically all political power lies with a central government
utilities Services needed by the public, such as water, gas, and electricity
zoning Local rules that divide a community into areas and tell how the land in each area can be used

Organization and Functions of State Government

Each of the 50 states has its own government. State governments carry out much of the work of meeting the needs of citizens. These governments have responsibility for public education, transportation, health, and safety.

State Government	Function and Significance
Executive agencies	State executive agencies carry out the day-to-day work of the executive branch. Departments of health, revenue, and natural resources are examples of executive agencies.
Executive officials	A team of executive officials assists the governor. These officials include the lieutenant governor, the secretary of state, the attorney general, and the state treasurer.
Governor	The governor's role of chief executive is similar to that of the President. Like the President, the governor also has legislative powers and certain judicial powers.
State courts	Tasks of the state courts involve hearing civil and criminal cases, but state courts also act as a check on the two other branches of state government.
State court judges	Judges are the foundation of the state court system and perform many of the duties of federal judges. State court judges are elected rather than appointed.
State legislators	Many state legislators are full-time lawmakers who must meet certain qualifications. In most states, legislators must be United States citizens and live in the state and district they represent. Seats in state legislatures are apportioned, or divided among districts, on the basis of equal representation.

Local Government

Local governments—such as those of counties, cities, and towns—are created by the states and have only those powers that state governments give them. Daily life runs on the services of local governments, such as garbage collection, road repair, and water supply.

Local Government	Function and Significance
Council-manager	The goal of the council-manager plan is to run city government like a business. The council is chosen through an election in which candidates have no political ties. The council makes ordinances and hires a city manager to handle day-to-day city business.
Commissioners	Under the commission plan, voters choose several commissioners who together make ordinances. In addition, each commissioner directs one of the city's departments, such as finance or public assistance.
County government	The county form of local government came to North America with the English colonists, as colonies were divided into counties to carry out laws in rural areas. Today, most counties help state governments keep law and order and collect taxes.
County officials	Most counties are governed by a county board, which sets up county programs and passes local laws. A well-known elected county official is the sheriff, who runs the county jail and enforces the law.
Mayor-council	About 35 percent of the cities in the United States use the mayor-council plan, which provides both an executive (mayor) and a legislative (council) branch for city government.
Departments of public safety	The police department, fire department, and other emergency services are run by the local government.
Special districts	A special district is a unit of government that generally provides a single service. It can serve one community or cover parts or all of several communities.
Tax collection	About 25 percent of local government revenue comes from property tax on land and buildings, and other money is collected through sales and income taxes.
Townships	In the Middle Atlantic states and in the Midwest, counties are often divided into townships. In many urban areas, townships elect representatives to serve on the county board.

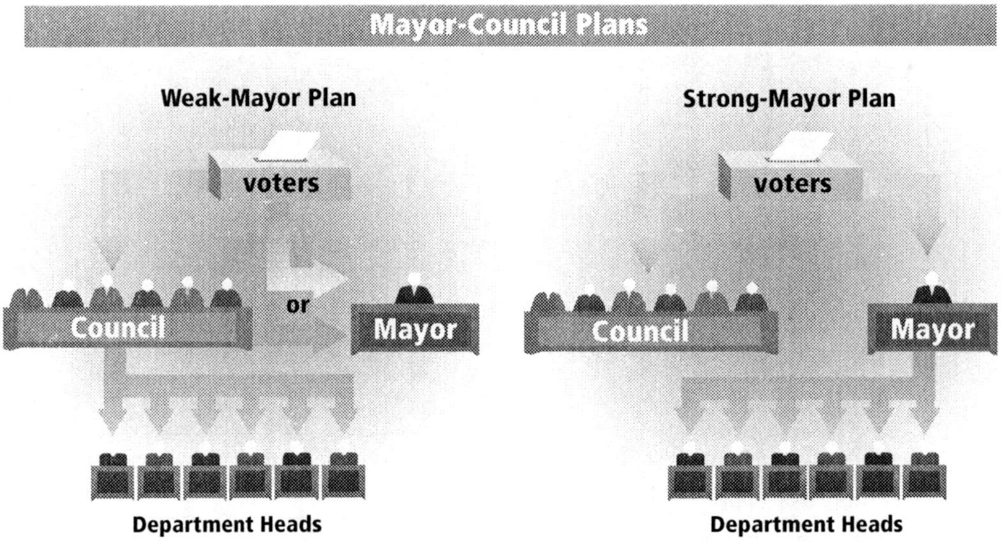

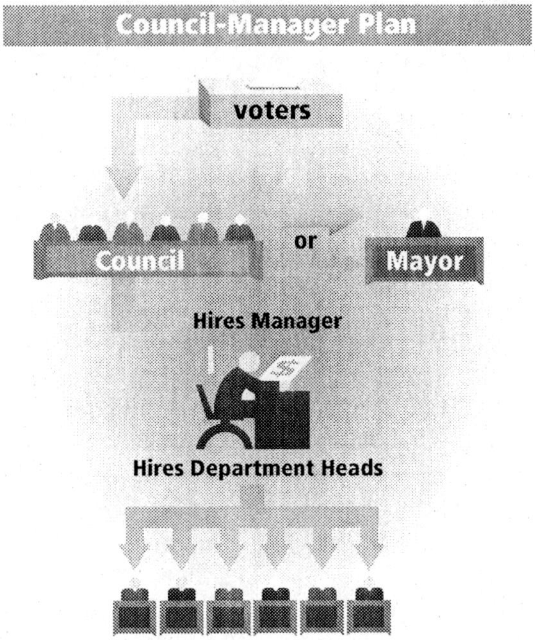
Council-Manager Plan
voters
Council
or
Mayor
Hires Manager
Hires Department Heads

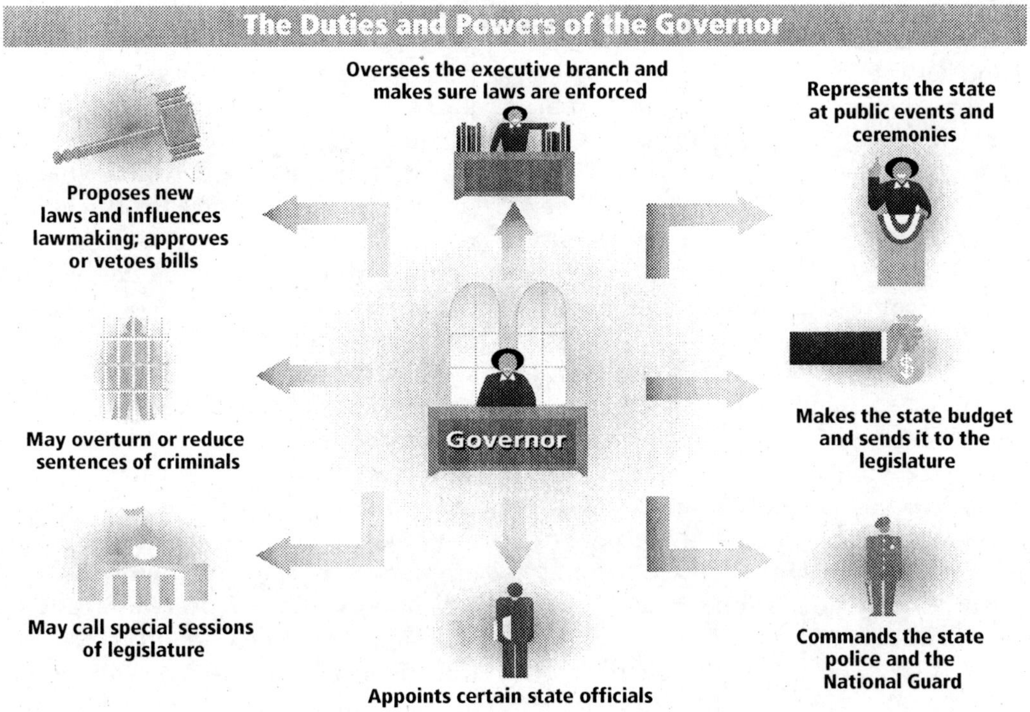
The Duties and Powers of the Governor
Oversees the executive branch and makes sure laws are enforced
Represents the state at public events and ceremonies
Proposes new laws and influences lawmaking; approves or vetoes bills
May overturn or reduce sentences of criminals
Governor
Makes the state budget and sends it to the legislature
May call special sessions of legislature
Commands the state police and the National Guard
Appoints certain state officials

Study Sheets

Unit 5 Foundations of Economics

Key Terms

boycott Refusal to buy
capital Anything produced in an economy that is used to produce other goods and services
capitalism A system in which people make their own decisions about how to save resources as capital, and how to use their capital to produce goods and provide services
career The occupation for which you train and which you pursue as your life's work
collective bargaining The process by which representatives of unions and business try to reach agreement about wages and working conditions
command economy The government or a central authority owns or controls the factors of production and makes the basic economic decisions
consumption The act of buying or using goods and services
corporation A business that is separate from the people who own it and legally acts as a single person
demand The amount of a product or service buyers are willing and able to buy at different prices
disposable income The amount of money left after taxes have been paid
distribution The process by which goods and services are made available to the people who want them
dividends Payments from the profits of companies in which they own stock
entrepreneur A person who starts a business
factors of production The resources people have for producing goods and services to satisfy their wants
fixed expenses Expenses that have to be paid regularly, usually every month, such as rent and car payments
free enterprise The system in which individuals in a market economy are free to undertake economic activities with little or no control by the government
fringe benefits Indirect payments for work
insurance A plan by which a company gives protection from the cost of injury or loss
interest Payment for the use of capital
invest Use of money to help a business get started or grow, with the hope that the business will earn a profit that can be shared
labor unions Organizations of workers that seek to improve wages and working conditions and to protect members' rights
liquidity The ability to turn savings back into cash
market economy A system in which private individuals own the factors of production and are free to make their own choices about production, distribution, and consumption
market price The price at which buyers and sellers agree to trade
mixed economy An economy that is a mixture of the three basic systems—traditional, command, and market
Occupational Outlook Handbook A guide published by the Department of Labor Bureau of Labor Statistics
partnership A type of business in which two or more people share ownership
profit The difference between what it costs to produce something and the price the buyer pays for it
opportunity cost The benefit given up when scarce resources are used for one purpose instead of another
scarcity Resources are always limited compared with the number and variety of wants people have
sole proprietorship A business owned by an individual
strike Workers' refusal to work unless employers meet certain demands
technology The practical application of science to commerce or industry
time deposit A savings plan with a set length of time keeping your money in the account
traditional economy The basic economic decisions are made according to long-established ways of behaving that are unlikely to change
variable expenses Expenses that change from month to month
warranty A manufacturer's promise to repair an item if it breaks within a certain time from the date of purchase

Three Types of Economics

Type	Description
Traditional	In a traditional economy, the basic economic decisions are made according to long-established ways of behaving that are unlikely to change. Because individuals or families in a traditional economy usually own their own resources, such as land, tools, and labor, they have some freedom to make their own day-to-day decisions about when and how to use their resources. They have little freedom, however, when it comes to making the basic economic decisions already set by tradition. As a result, there is very little change in the economy over time.
Command	In a command economy, the government or a central authority owns or controls the factors of production and makes the basic economic decisions. In such a system, the government usually has charge of important parts of the economy, such as transportation, communication, banking, and manufacturing. Farms and many stores are government-controlled. The government may also set wages and decide who will work at which jobs.
Market	In a market economy, private individuals own the factors of production and are free to make their own choices about production, distribution, and consumption. In a market economy, all economic decisions are made through a kind of bargaining process that takes place in markets. The value of what you have to offer sets the value of what you get. Therefore, no one person or group runs a market economy. Instead, everyone takes part in running it by freely making economic decisions.

Common Savings Plans

Way to Save	Description
Insurance	Investment can be made in an insurance policy such as life insurance. After a set number of years, certain kinds of policies can be surrendered for cash value, plus interest.
Interest-Bearing Checking	The owner of these accounts (called NOW or Negotiable Order of Withdrawal accounts) can write checks on the account, which also earns interest.
Mutual Fund	These are pooled funds of investors, managed by a professional. Funds usually are invested in stocks and bonds.
Passbook Savings	These plans usually pay a fixed interest rate, and money can be withdrawn at any time.
Real Estate	This involves the purchase of land and/or buildings. Some people earn income from the rent they charge for living and working spaces. Profit can be made when real estate is sold for a higher price than was paid for it and when rent charged exceeds the amount owned for the property.
Savings Bond	Savings bonds are sold by the government. It is common for bonds to be sold for half of their full value, reaching their full value after a period of time.
Stock	Stocks are shares in corporations. Owners of stock sometimes earn income from dividends. Owners make profits when they sell their stock for a higher price than what they paid for it.
Time Deposit	These are funds deposited for a set period of time that usually carries a penalty for early withdrawal. The interest rate depends on the time limit on deposit.

Unit 6 Government and the Economy

Key Terms

balanced budget A requirement that governments do not spend more than the tax revenues they receive

bartering Exchanging goods and services

Board of Governors Group responsible for running the Federal Reserve System as a whole

business cycle A repeated series of "ups" of growth and "downs" of recession

currency The coins and paper bills used as money in an economy

deficit The amount by which government spending is greater than government income

deficit budget Result of government spending more than the tax revenue it receives

demand deposit The money in a checking account

direct tax A tax on income

economic freedom The freedom to own property, to make a profit, and to make choices about what to produce, buy, and sell

economic growth An increase in the production of goods and services, which provides citizens with a higher standard of living

entitlement programs Governmental programs that provide benefits to people entitled by law to receive them

federal budget The government's plan for how it will raise and spend money

Federal Reserve System System that provides important services to United States banks and regulates their activities

fiscal policy A government's decisions about the amount of money it spends and the amount it collects in taxes

fractional reserve banking Banking practice that keeps a percentage of checking and savings deposits in reserve, with the rest of the money available for loans and investments

full employment No person who wants to work should be out of a job

gross domestic product (GDP) The total dollar value of all final goods and services produced within the country in a year

indirect tax Part of the price a consumer pays for a product

inflation A general rise in the price level of goods and services

loan An amount of money borrowed for a certain time period

mixed economy System that includes the private sector (the market sector) and the public sector (government).

monetary policy Regulation of the money supply by the Federal Reserve System

money supply The total amount of money available for use as a medium of exchange

monopoly When a single business has the power to control prices in a market

national debt The total amount of money the government owes to lenders

national income accounting Process by which our nation keeps track of our overall income and spending

progressive tax Takes a higher percentage of taxes from a person with a higher income than it does from a person with a lower income

proportional tax Requires each taxpayer to pay the same proportion, or percentage, of their income as taxes

recession A slowdown in economic activity and production

regressive tax Takes a larger percentage of tax on income from a person with a lower income than from a person with a higher income

surplus The amount by which government income is greater than government spending

surplus budget The result of government spending less than it receives in tax revenues

trust A group of several companies organized to benefit from the high prices they all agree to charge

Government Intervention in the Economy

Service	Description
Regulates business	The government passes laws that establish rules for business conduct. For example, it can limit the number of hours workers are required to work in one day, or set safety rules for airplanes. The government also can establish regulatory agencies to enforce these laws.
Makes direct payments to individuals	The government can give money to people who need help to pay for food, shelter, medical care, and other basic needs.
Owns resources and produces goods and services	The government can own land, such as the national forests. It also can run businesses that promote the common good, such as providing hydroelectric power from a government-built dam.
Helps pay for important economic activities	The government can give a sum of money to a private business to help it provide an important product or service. For example, the federal government has given money to help farmers, airlines, and builders of housing for the poor.
Controls the amount of money spent and the amount received in taxes	The government imposes taxes that take money back from the economy, and spending puts it back. By controlling the in-and-out flow of taxes and spending, governments can influence how the economy performs. In addition, the federal government can control the total supply of money.
Makes tax rules and collect special taxes	The government can change the rates at which people's incomes are taxed, and it can make tax rules that reward certain economic activities and punish others.

Bank Services

Service	Description
Checking accounts	Checks are used by people who have deposited money in a checking account at a bank. The money in a checking account is called a demand deposit. Checks are used to pay for goods, to pay bills, and are safe because they are specific to the person whose name is printed on them; they provide a good record of how people spend their money.
Savings accounts	Money in a savings account is not a demand deposit and cannot be withdrawn on demand. However, banks pay interest on money in a savings account because it uses the money for its own investments. Savings are an important source of funds in our economy. With savings funds, banks can make loans to help people in the economy buy goods and services and to help businesses produce goods and services.
Loans	Money borrowed for a certain amount of time. People who take out loans have decided that the benefit of having money now is greater than the cost of paying it back with interest later. By making loans, banks serve an important function. They help businessess make use of productive resources, which causes the economy to grow.

Sources of Federal Revenue

Source	Description
Income taxes	The largest part of the federal government's revenue comes from income taxes. Individuals pay two kinds of federal tax on their incomes: personal income tax and social security tax. The amount of personal income tax you pay is based on a percentage that increases as your income grows. Social security tax is also based on a percentage of your income, but it does not vary according to income.
Excise Taxes	Taxes charged on specific products, such as cigarettes, alcohol, gasoline, jewels, and furs, are called excise taxes. In addition to raising money, many excise taxes are intended to regulate certain kinds of consumption.
Tariffs, fees, and sales	The federal government collects about four percent of its revenue from various other sources. Tariffs are taxes on imported products. Fees are charges to users of certain services, such as visitors to national parks. The government may sell resources to make money.

Characteristics of a Good Tax

Economical	The government should not spend too much money to collect the tax.
Good reason	Taxpayers must know that their tax revenues will serve a purpose, even if they do not agree with every aspect of government spending.
Fair and equitable	The Benefits-Received Principle says that the benefits of the tax should go to the people who pay the tax. For example, the gasoline tax is fair because the more gas a driver buys, the more miles he or she travels on government-provided highways. The Ability-to-Pay Principle, usually applied to income taxes, says that a citizen should pay taxes in relation to how much he or she is able to pay.
Certain	Taxpayers must know when the tax is due and exactly how much they must pay.
Convenient	The tax should be simple and convenient for the taxpayer to pay and for the government to collect.

Types of Government Budgets

Balanced Budget	Most states and local governments require this kind of budget whereby governments do not spend more than the revenues they receive. When the economy weakens and tax revenues drop, spending must be cut to keep the budget balanced.
Deficit Budget	Governments spend more that the tax revenues they receive. The federal government must borrow money to make up the difference between spending and revenue. The government can sell bonds to borrow the money.
Surplus Budget	Governments spend less than they receive in tax revenues. Surplus revenues were used in the late 1990s and early 2000s to pay back money borrowed during deficit budget years.

Unit 7 The American Legal System

Key Terms

answer The defendant's written response to a complaint

arbitration The use of a third person to make a legal decision that is binding on all parties

arraignment A court hearing in which the defendant is formally charged with a crime and enters a plea of guilty, not guilty, or no contest

assault Placing someone in fear with or without actual physical contact

bail Money that a defendant pays the court as a kind of promise that he or she will return for the trial

battery Harming someone with physical contact

burglary The act of breaking into a building and planing to do something illegal inside

civil disobedience Breaking a law in a nonviolent way because it goes against personal morals

civil law The group of laws that help settle disagreements between people

common law A body of law based on judges' decisions

compensation Being "made whole" for harm caused by another person's acts

complaint A legal document that charges someone with having caused harm

contracts Legal agreements between buyers and sellers

crime Any behavior that is illegal because the government considers it harmful to society

criminal law The group of laws that tell which acts are crimes, how accused persons should be tried in court, and how crimes should be punished

damages Money that is paid in an effort to make up for a loss

delinquent A juvenile who is found guilty of a crime

deposition The record of answers to questions asked of a witness before a trial

discovery The process of gathering evidence before a trial

embezzlement Stealing money that has been trusted to your care

equity The use of general rules of fairness to settle conflicts

felony A serious crime for which the penalty can be imprisonment for more than one year

indictment A formal charge against the accused

injunction An order to do or not do a certain act

laws Rules that are enforced by governments

lawsuits Cases in which a court is asked to settle a dispute

legal code A written collection of laws, often organized by subject

mediation A process by which people agree to use a third party to help them settle a conflict

misdemeanor A less serious crime for which the penalty is often a fine

morals Beliefs about what is fair and what is right or wrong

parole Letting an inmate go free to serve the rest of his or her sentence outside of prison

plea bargaining Agreeing to plead guilty in exchange for a lesser charge or a lighter sentence

probable cause A good reason to believe that a suspect has been involved in a crime

small claims court A civil court that people use when the amount of money they want to recover is small, usually not more than $3,000

status offender A youth who is found guilty of breaking a law that applies only to young people

statutes Written laws made by legislatures

summons An order to appear in court

subpoena A court order to produce a witness or document

terrorism A crime in which people or groups of people use, or say they will use, violence in order to get what they want from the government or society

treason The betrayal of one's country by helping its enemies or by making war against it

warrant A legal paper, issued by a court, giving police permission to make an arrest, seizure, or search

Why We Have Laws

The need for order	One of the most basic purposes of laws is to bring order to society. One way laws bring order is by telling people what they may or may not do.
The need to protect people's safety	No society can run smoothly if people live in constant fear. Therefore, physical attacks, such as murder and rape, are against the law. Laws also protect the quality of people's lives.
The need to protect people's property	Laws against stealing are one way in which the government protects people's property; property includes ideas and inventions. Laws also give you rights if your property is damaged.
The need to protect individual freedoms	The Bill of Rights makes it illegal for the government to deny freedom of religion, freedom of speech, freedom of the press, and other basic freedoms.
The need to promote the common good	The Preamble of the Constitution declares that one of the goals of our government is to promote the general welfare, which means the common good of the people. Therefore, there are laws that protect society as a whole, such as laws that protect the environment and everyone's health.

Where Our Laws Come From

Rules written by legislatures	Laws that are written by Congress or by state legislatures are called statutes. Laws made by city or town councils are called ordinances. A federal law or a federal statute is a law that everyone in the nation must obey. Ordinances only apply to that state or local community.
Decisions made by judges	Judges do not write laws. They decide cases based on laws that already exist. If a case comes up with no precedent, a judge then makes a new decision that reflects current beliefs and customs.
Legal codes	Lawmakers have organized many laws into legal codes in order to keep track of them. Codes provide a way to organize laws so that they are up-to-date and easy for people to find.
Constitutions	The United States Constitution and the constitutions of the states are collections of laws that include the basic rules by which our governments are run. State laws must follow the state constitution. Local, state, and federal laws must all follow the United States Constitution.

Kinds of Laws

Criminal	Criminal laws protect society as a whole. Crimes are divided into two categories: felonies and misdemeanors. Congress decides which types of behavior will be considered crimes anywhere in the United States. Each state legislature can make its own criminal laws as long as they do not come into conflict with federal statutes or the Constitution.
Civil	Civil laws provide a way for people to settle disagreements in court. The government does not automatically get involved.

Police

Local police	Local police officers patrol neighborhoods, find stolen property, investigate complaints, arrest lawbreakers, help solve disputes, and write traffic tickets.
State police	The job of state police varies from state to state. In many states their major job is to protect automobile drivers and enforce traffic laws on state highways.
Federal law enforcement	Agencies such as the Federal Bureau of Investigation (FBI) help the local police with such problems as gang wars and drug dealing. The FBI also enforces federal laws, such as those against bank robbery and kidnapping.

Types of Civil Cases

Property cases	People often want payment for damage to their property. Another common type of property case involves charges of trespassing. Property cases may be settled through compensation or through equity.
Consumer cases	Questions related to the rights of consumers are covered in a collection of laws called the Uniform Commercial Code. Many of these laws set basic rules for contracts. The buyer promises to pay for a product or service, and the seller agrees that it will meet certain standards. Conflicts arise when either a buyer or a seller says that the other has not lived up to the contract.
Domestic relations cases	Cases that concern family relationships are called domestic relations cases, most of which relate to divorce.
Housing cases	Housing cases involve relationships between landlords and tenants. Under civil law, a tenant and a landlord may take certain steps if either one believes that the other has not lived up to the lease. In cases of housing law, the courts must consider the rights and responsibilities of both landlords and tenants.
Probate cases	Disagreements may arise over how to divide up the property of a friend or relative who has died. Such cases are called probate cases. Usually probate cases involve questions over whether a person's will can be trusted.

Types of Crime

Against people	Acts that threaten, hurt, or end a person's life; these include murder, rape, and assault
Against property	These include stealing, arson, and vandalism; there are three kinds of stealing: larceny, robbery, and burglary
White-collar	These are nonviolent acts for personal or business gain; they include fraud, embezzlement, and tax evasion
Victimless	Acts that hurt no one except the people who commit them; they include drug use and gambling
Against Government	These acts include treason and terrorism

What Happens to Someone Who is Arrested

Arrest	The police have probable cause to believe a suspect has been involved in a crime.
Preliminary hearing	The prosecutor must show the judge that a crime has been committed and that there is enough evidence against the defendant to go ahead with the case. The judge may decide to dismiss the case if the prosecutor cannot show enough evidence to connect the defendant to the crime. The judge may set bail.
Grand jury	The grand jury reviews cases involving serious federal crimes and decides if there is probable cause for believing that the defendant committed the crime. The grand jury either returns an indictment or refuses to indict.
Felony arraignment	A defendant who is indicted must appear before a court hearing in which the defendant is formally charged with a crime and enters a plea of guilty, not guilty, or no contest.
Pretrial motions	Steps taken by the defendant and his or her attorney before the actual trial begins to suppress evidence.
Plea bargaining	The defendant agrees to plead guilty in exchange for a lesser charge or a lighter sentence. The defendant gets a milder punishment and the government saves the time and cost of a trial. Most criminal cases never go to trial.

Going to Trial

Jury selection	Citizens are called to serve on a jury. Both the prosecution and the defense look for people who will listen carefully to the evidence presented and make up their minds fairly.
Trial	A jury must decide if the defendant is guilty "beyond a reasonable doubt" by carefully studying the evidence. The defendant has the right not to answer questions. The trial must be speedy and public.
Sentencing	If a defendant is found guilty, the final step in the courtroom is his or her punishment.

The Juvenile Court Process

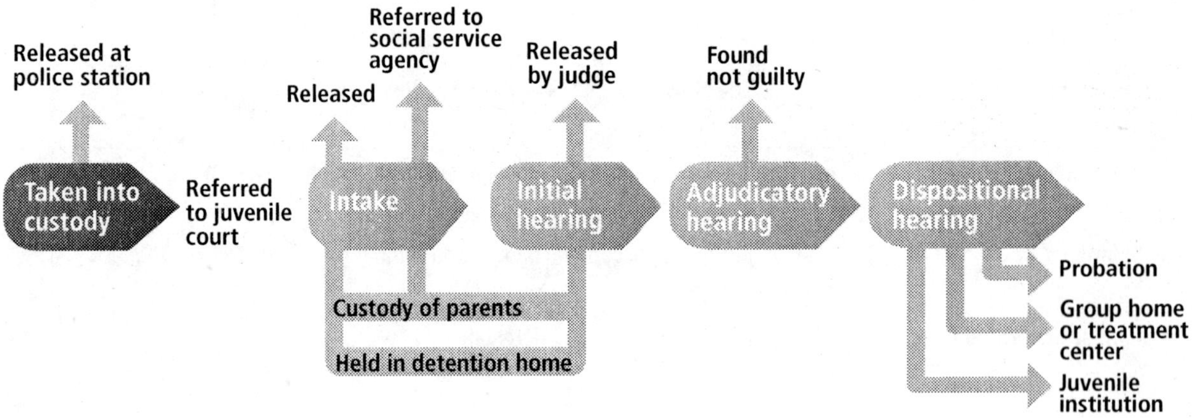

Unit 8 People Make a Difference

Key Terms

bias Favoring of one point of view

campaign manager Person who helps plan the broad outlines of the campaign

campaign press secretary Person who makes certain that the news shows the candidate in the best light

canvass Going door-to-door handing out information and asking people which candidates they support

caucus A meeting of party leaders to discuss issues or choose candidates

closed primary A primary in which a voter must be registered as a party member and may vote only in that party's primary

direct mail A way of sending messages to large groups of people through the mail

direct primary An election in which members of a political party choose candidates to run for office in the name of the party

electors People who promise to cast votes for the candidate selected by voters

general election An election in which voters make final decisions about candidates and issues

incumbent Someone who already holds the office for which he or she is running

independent voter People who do not support a particular political party

media Television, radio, newspapers, and magazines

nominate The party's naming of candidates to run for public office

open primary A primary in which voters do not need to declare a party before voting, but may vote in only one party's primary

patronage The system in which party leaders do favors for loyal supporters of the party

planks Position statements on each specific issue in a party's platform

platform A statement of a party's official stand on major public issues

political party An organization of citizens who wish to influence and control government by getting their members elected to office

precincts Voting districts

propaganda A message that is meant to influence people's ideas, opinions, or actions in a certain way

registration The process of signing up to be a voter

self-nomination Declaring that you are running for office

split ticket The practice of voting for candidates of more than one party on the same ballot

straight ticket The practice of voting for the candidates of only one party

write-in candidate One who asks voters to write his or her name on the ballot

Political Party Organizational Structure

The Democratic and Republican parties are set up similarly. Both parties have local, state, and national organizations. These organizations work independently of one another. In other words, no single authority makes decisions for the whole party.

Structure	Description
Party members	Individual members at the local level are the most important part of any party. These members do the job of getting the party's candidates elected.
Precinct organization	Each community is divided into precincts, or voting districts. In each precinct, each party has a chairperson or captain who organizes volunteers to try to get as many party members as possible to vote.
City and county committees	Parties at the local level elect members to city and county committees. These committees may recommend candidates for office and are responsible for running local campaigns.
State committees	Each party is also organized at the state level. Most states have party committees, each with a chairperson. At state conventions, party leaders write the state party platform and nominate candidates for office. Party leaders also raise money and help with candidates' campaigns.
National committee	Once every four years, each party holds a national convention. At the convention, delegates write the national party platform and nominate the candidates for President and Vice President. Between national conventions, the national committee keeps the party running. During election years, the national committee helps the candidates for President and Vice President run their campaigns. It also works to elect members of Congress and to raise funds for the party.

Steps for Voting

Registration	The process of signing up to vote, which was introduced in the late 1800s. In most states, registration occurs several weeks before the election. Each state makes its own laws about voter registration.
Voting—when and where	An act of Congress set the Tuesday after the first Monday in November as the day for federal congressional and presidential elections. Most elections for state offices take place at the same time. Primary elections and elections for local governments may take place at any time during the year, but most are set for the spring. Voting takes place in what are called polling places, each of which serves a voting district or precinct.
How to cast a vote	On entering the polling place, you check in with an election official, who looks up your name to confirm that you are registered to vote there. Depending on where you live, you may pull a lever on an election machine, mark an X on a paper ballot, punch a hole in a card, or make your choice on a touchpad similar to an ATM. If you will not be able to get to a polling place on election day, you can ask to have an absentee ballot sent to your home.

How Political Parties Help Government

Selecting candidates	Parties take the responsibility for finding and nominating qualified candidates.
Setting goals	Parties establish positions on issues and set goals for government.
Providing leadership	Parties help provide day-to-day leadership necessary to make laws and carry out programs.
Acting as "watchdogs"	The party not in power makes sure that the public knows when the party in power is not living up to its promises. The parties also keep tabs on each other.

Propaganda Techniques

Glittering Generalities
Use words and phrases that sound appealing and that everyone agrees with.
Example: "I stand for freedom and the American way."

Card Stacking
Use only those facts that support your argument.
Example: "My opponent voted against raising Social Security." (You do not mention that she voted no because the proposed increase was too small.)

Plain Folks
Tell voters that you are just like them—an ordinary person with similar needs and ideas.
Example: "I've lived in this city all my life. My children go to the same schools as your children."

Name Calling
Attach negative labels to your opponent.
Example: "He's soft on crime."

Bandwagon
Appeals to desire to follow the crowd.
Example: "Polls show that more than 80 percent of voters support me."

Transfer
Connect yourself to a respected person, group, or symbol.
Example: "Remember what Abraham Lincoln said..."

Formation of Third Parties

Reason	• to support a cause or idea • to back a candidate who split from a main party
Problems	• difficulty getting on the ballot because of election laws in many states that favor the two major parties • lack of financial support • lack of confidence from voters
Importance	• can change the outcome of an election by drawing votes away from one of the main parties • can bring up new ideas or press for action on certain issues

Unit 9 The United States and the World

Key Terms

aggression An attack or threat of attack by another country

balance of power The threat that one superpower's military strength might be used against the other's

bureaucracy A structure of departments staffed by nonelected government officials

Cold War A struggle between the United States and the Soviet Union much like a real war but with no armed battles

colony A territory ruled by a more powerful nation called a colonial power

communism System in which the central government owns and controls the economic resources

containment A policy of using military power and money to prevent the spread of communism

détente A laxing of tensions between the United States and the Soviet Union

deterrence Keeping a strong defense to discourage aggression by other nations

diplomacy Relations and communications carried out between countries

foreign aid A program of giving military and economic help to other countries

intelligence Information about another country and what its government plans to do

isolationism A foreign policy that seeks to limit relations with other countries as much as possible

nationalism A pride the people of a nation feel in their shared history and a loyalty to their nation

National Security Advisor Director of the National Security Council

National Security Council (NSC) Group that advises the President on the country's safety

neutrality A policy of not taking sides in wars between other countries

peacekeepers Members of the military whose job is usually to help settle conflicts and maintain order in a region

sanctions Measures to stop or limit trade with another nation in order to change its behavior

sovereignty The power to make and carry out laws within a nation's borders

standard of living The number and kinds of goods and services people can have

summit meeting A meeting at which the President discusses important issues with heads of other governments

Approaches to American Foreign Policy

Many people and organizations have ideas about America's relations with other countries. They want the government to take action to help achieve their goals.

Group or Entity	Involvement in Foreign Policy
Congress	The Senate has the power to approve or reject treaties. The President's choices for the diplomatic corps must be approved by the Senate. Only Congress has the power to declare war.
Department of Defense	Advises the President and oversees the armed forces
Department of State	Advises the President on foreign policy and carries out foreign policy once that policy has been made.
National Security Council (NSC)	The NSC advises the President on the country's safety. The NSC meets when a crisis arises and American security seems in danger.
The President	The President shapes foreign policy both as commander-in-chief of the armed forces and as the nation's chief diplomat. The President sets defense policies, meets with leaders of other countries, and makes treaties and executive agreements.
Private Groups	Private organizations such as business groups, labor groups, and political groups also can shape foreign policy by lobbying Congress and the President.

Goals of Foreign Policy

National security	to keep the nation safe from attack or harm is the chief goal, mainly focused on the threat of war
World peace	to encourage countries to work together as a way to avoid war
Trade	to increase trade because it creates markets for American goods and services, bringing greater interdependence and therefore cooperation
Human rights and democracy	to encourage all countries to respect the human rights of freedom, justice, and equality

Tools of Foreign Policy

Defense	helps the government maintain national security
Alliances	form military, political, or economic ties with other countries
Diplomacy	settles disagreements with other countries peacefully; makes alliances and trade agreements; usually carried out by the Department of State
Foreign aid	gives military and economic help to other countries; helps strengthen governments and political groups that are friendly to the United States
Trade measures	use quotas, tariffs, and sanctions to regulate trade with other countries; goals are to get other countries to buy American goods and to support us in other foreign policy goals
Intelligence	gathers information in order to help meet the goal of national security

International Organizations

As nations of the world have grown more interdependent, permanent organizations have been set up to deal with the world's problems.

Organization	Description
Association of Southeast Asian Nations (ASEAN)	ASEAN works for economic and political cooperation in the Southeast Asian region.
European Union (EU)	Formed by the nations of Western Europe to break down barriers to trade and travel in their region. In 1999, 11 EU countries adopted a new, single currency—the euro.
North Atlantic Treaty Organization (NATO)	Defensive alliance formed by the nations of Western Europe and the United States for mutual protection against the Soviet Union and communism after World War II.
Organization of American States (OAS)	OAS works for economic and political cooperation. It is an alliance made up of countries in North, Central, and South America.
Organization of African Unity (OAU)	OAU works for economic and political cooperation in Africa.
North American Free Trade Agreement (NAFTA)	NAFTA lowered trade barriers between Canada, Mexico, and the United States.
United Nations	An organization that includes most countries in the world. The UN works to promote peace, cooperation, and development throughout the world.

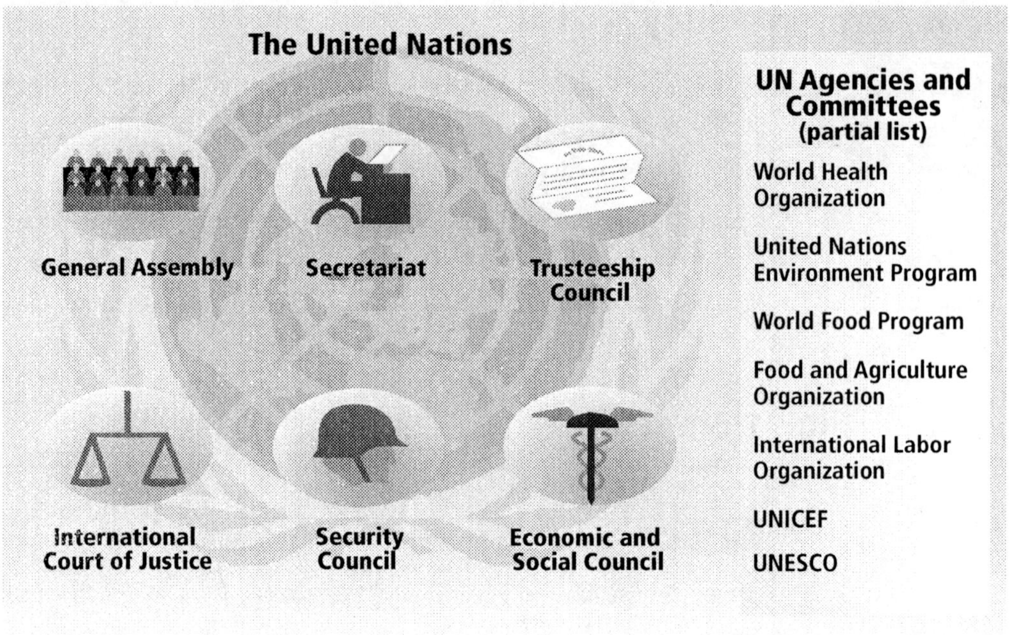

Global Problems

Problem	Description
Limited natural resources	Earth has limited natural resources; our main natural resources are water, air, soil, trees and other plants, animals, sunlight, and minerals. Population growth and some lifestyles put a strain on these resources.
Pollution	Pollution makes the environment unclean and unhealthy. Toxic chemicals, acid rain, the greenhouse effect, and the weakening of the ozone layer are threatening the world.
The arms buildup	A number of countries now have the power to wage a nuclear war that could destroy life on earth as we know it. Some countries have large amounts of nerve gas and other chemical weapons.
Terrorism	Terrorism is the use or threat of violence to spread fear, usually for the purpose of reaching political goals. Terrorists can strike anywhere, in any country, making their attacks hard to prevent.
Violations of human rights	Violation of human rights in one country is a global issue when refugees flee across borders. People who seek to protect human rights face two challenges: to find out where violations are taking place and to find ways to make governments stop the violations.

Regional Challenges

Region	Challenge
Africa	Many countries of Africa are among the poorest in the world. Many also suffer from political instability. During the 1990s, civil wars raged in Sudan, Rwanda, the Congo Republic, and Algeria, leaving hundreds of thousands dead. Foreign policy questions for Africa are similar to those for other parts of the developing world.
Eastern Europe	The Czech Republic, Hungary, and Poland have made great strides toward democratic government and free market economies. The standard of living in Eastern Europe, however, is still well below that of Western Europe. Wars in Bosnia and Serbia have left serious ethnic divisions that will need to be healed.
Latin America	During the Cold War, the United States used aid, diplomacy, and military intervention to stop the spread of communism in Latin America. By the early 1990s, most Latin American countries were governed by fragile democracies.
The Middle East	In 2000, violence broke out once again between Israelis and Palestinians. It will take a great effort to overcome the long history of religious and political conflict in the region.